The Last Stand

The Last Stand

RALPH NADER'S STUDY GROUP REPORT
ON THE NATIONAL FORESTS

Daniel R. Barney

GROSSMAN PUBLISHERS, New York, 1974

To
Mother and Dad

The Study Group

Daniel R. Barney, Editor and Author
  A.B., Harvard College (1972); 2nd-year law student, University of Texas at Austin
Hale Andrews, Writer
  A.B., Harvard College (1971)
Henry Drummonds, Writer
  A.B., University of Oregon (1969); J.D., Harvard Law School (1972)
J. Lawrence Schultz, Research Director
  A.B., Yale College (1967); J.D., Harvard Law School (1970)
Ann Clark
  A.B., Smith College (1965), Ph.D. in Philosophy, University of Texas at Austin (1970)
John Cowell
  A.B., University of Arkansas (1968)
Ruth Glushien
  A.B., Harvard College (1972)
James S. Henry
  A.B., Harvard College (1972)
Larry MacDonnell
  A.B., University of Michigan (1966); J.D., University of Denver Law School (1972)
Bonnie Temple
  A.B., Radcliffe (1963); M.U.P., New York University (1971); 3rd-year law student, Georgetown University
Monica Wilch
  B.S. (1970); M.S. in Journalism (1971), Northwestern University
Connie Jo Smith, Production
Ruth C. Fort, Production

A forest is not solely so many thousand feet of lumber to be logged when markets make it profitable. It is an integral part of our natural land covering, and the most potent factor in maintaining Nature's delicate balance in the organic and inorganic worlds. . . . Such public necessities, therefore, must not be destroyed because there is profit for someone in their destruction. The preservation of the forests must be lifted above mere dollars and cents considerations.

—President Franklin D. Roosevelt, in a speech drafted by officials of the Forest Service, January 29, 1935

Contents

Introduction by Ralph Nader

The National Forests, covering ten percent of the nation's land area, are America's last natural frontier. Like other frontiers of the American past, the Forests, if managed prudently, could contribute greatly to the quality as well as quantity of American life. Already, for a public weary of the frustrations and ugliness of urban life, they offer a primeval haven of open space. As a corrective for polluted air, lakes, and streams, the Forests serve as critical nourishers and filters. They are in many areas the last refuge for grizzlies, the American bald eagle, and other endangered species. And for the $43 billion wood products industry, which leveled most of the valuable timber once standing on private lands, they are the last reservoir of softwood timber left to be drained.

Recognizing the conflicting values involved in these alternative uses of National Forests, Congress in 1960 enacted guidelines for their management which established the principles of *multiple use* and *sustained yield*. Multiple use demanded the general balancing of timber production with use of the forests for recreation, watershed, wildlife protection, and other nonlogging activities. The sustained-yield objective was to ensure that the timber harvest from National Forests did not exceed the renewal capacity of the forests, and thus to prevent a net depletion of the nation's forest resources.

The U.S. Forest Service presides over the National Forests. Although many of its officials model themselves after Gifford Pinchot, the Service's progressive and legendary founder, the Service as a whole has come to observe only rhetorically the principles of multiple use and sustained yield. Coached by the Nixon White House's heavy courtship of the timber industry, the Forest Service has succumbed increasingly to industry schemes to convert much of the National Forests to timber factories, permanently damaging their recreation potential. The Forest Service, pressured by the Agriculture, Housing, and Interior Secretaries of the

Nixon Cabinet, is considering a plan to increase timber production from the National Forests by fifty percent in the next ten years. The Service also plans nearly to double the 198,000 miles of permanent roads in the Forests and to permit cutting of the last substantial unlogged old-growth forests in the United States. Much of the increased logging will be accomplished through clearcutting—the forester's version of General Sherman's "scorched earth" warfare. Large tracts will be completely stripped of trees, then set afire to destroy logging debris, and finally *scarified*—the earth scraped bare with bulldozers—to prepare it for planting.

As this report clearly shows, the economic rationale for this plan—more National Forest timber equals lower lumber prices equals more housing starts—is seriously flawed. The cost of lumber makes up only nine percent of the fully financed cost of the average single-family dwelling, and housing starts historically have not increased as lumber prices declined. The economic alternatives to increased logging of the National Forests are discussed in detail in this report.

The proposals to increase so drastically the logging of National Forests come at a time when Americans are clamoring for more open space and recreation facilities. Campgrounds in state and federal parks are jammed and the most popular parks, like Yellowstone, may soon be restricted to visits "by reservation." According to the National Park Service, visits to National Parks will increase by over fifty percent in the next ten years. The National Park System is too small to absorb this human tide without drastic alterations in its character (witness recent proposals to build more roads and paved parking areas in Yellowstone, where automobile visits are often little more than a bucolic version of the commuter's freeway crawl, with a few panhandling bears to break the monotony).

The National Forests are the last undeveloped refuge for Americans' wanderlust. An increasing population, rising disposable income and leisure, and a growing interest in the natural environment are accelerating demands for new recreation areas. The National Forests will be the focus of this pressure for recreation expansion. Already vacationers spend more days at National Forests than at the

National Parks and most other public recreation areas combined. The National Forests are ideally suited for those
recreation activities where public participation is increasing the fastest—walking for pleasure, swimming, sightseeing, boating, camping, hiking, and bird watching.

Despite the good intentions of many top administrators
and agency foresters, the Forest Service has failed to manage the National Forests so as to satisfy America's spiraling
recreation needs. Its eagerness to accelerate timber production and its stubborn devotion to clearcutting mock the
principle of multiple-use management, intended to keep
timber production in harmony with recreation and other
nontimber uses of National Forests. Moreover, as this study
convincingly shows, the Forest Service has persistently
dragged its feet in preserving additional wild lands as
Wilderness Areas. In some cases the agency has actually
engaged in wilderness prevention, by building roads and
logging to disqualify areas slated for wilderness designation.

The National Forests, like the nation's lakes, rivers, and
oceans, are vulnerable to corporate interest groups eager to
exploit them for short-term economic gain. Just as labor
unions and local governments nationwide resist pollution
control because of their economic bondage to one dominant
industry, many residents of western states resist cutbacks
in National Forest logging because they make their living
in timber-related industries increasingly dependent on National Forest timber. The protection of National Forests,
like that of lakes and rivers, suffers from the lack of indices
to measure ecological, aesthetic, and recreational values
anywhere near as precise as the indices used to measure
the economic benefits of pollution and clearcutting. How
does one value the crucial ecological lifesaving of these
forests for Americans? How does one quantify the city
dweller's delight in a forest of stately old trees, the sense of
historical continuity and mystery that emanates from a
centuries-old forest, the preservation of habitat for endangered species, or the camper's thrill at the silence and
freshness of the deep woods? Not surprisingly, Congress
favors timber production over these other values because it
yields dollars for the federal treasury and votes and campaign contributions for its members. The sale of National

Forest timber returns over $350 milion a year to the U.S. Treasury. Recreation fees by contrast return less than $5 million. Incentives to treat National Forests as timber factories have been institutionalized in the fiscal planning of local governments as well. For example, to compensate counties which cannot tax National Forest land within their boundaries, the federal government pays them twenty-five percent of receipts from National Forest timber sales to support construction of public schools and roads.

The National Forests are uniquely vulnerable in other ways. A polluted river is a very public disgrace, but destroyed forests are often hidden away in our wilderness areas, undiscovered until the rising tide of recreationists spills over into their blasted acres—after it's too late for remedies. While rivers and lakes now have a federal agency —the Environmental Protection Agency—whose primary mission is to protect them, National Forests are "protected" by the Forest Service, whose primary mission is presently to increase timber production. The Congressional committees that approve budgets and pass legislation for the National Forests are ruled by the same bias. Almost every Forest Service decision resolves for better or worse a value conflict. When abuses occur, as in West Virginia's Monongahela National Forest in 1964, their consequences endure for generations. A river, once the sources of pollution have been cut off, begins cleansing itself immediately. A forest, once it has been clearcut and reseeded, is lost as a recreational resource for decades. If the forest is primeval, with stately trees centuries old, it is likely to be lost forever.

The bureaucracy entrusted with management of our National Forests has clearly benefited from the consciousness-raising of environmental groups, notably the Sierra Club, in the last three years. But its efforts to keep recreation and wildlife uses of the forests in harmony with timber production, as tardy and tentative as they have been, have been crippled further by pressure from the White House on behalf of logging interests. No agri-business interest group has found the doors to the White House more open than the timber industry. In 1969, when a coalition of environmental groups defeated the National Timber Supply Act with its goal of increasing the timber harvest from public lands by fifty percent, the logging and forest products industry lobbyists went to Presidential assistant Charles Colson, and had the same purpose achieved through executive action.

The Office of Management and Budget has consistently stymied efforts by the Forest Service to devote more resources to recreation development, wildlife habitat, and wilderness protection. As this report points out, a quick review of the Forest Service budget gives one the impression of examining a major logging company's financial statement. The Forest-Service-as-timber-company devotes over two-thirds of its $500-million annual budget to activities promoting timber production. When the Forest Service has attempted to remedy this imbalance, it has been silenced by the OMB.

The Last Stand is a disturbing case study of Congressional default and Presidential gamesmanship with special interests; it also suggests that the Forest Service's leadership, if its conservationist impulses were given more public support, would work to reduce the dominance of the loggers in the management of National Forests. The public forests are a great but fragile national treasure. If their fate is left to the forestry experts and timber interests by an uninformed public, then citizens concerned with the nation's ecological health, campers, hikers, wildlife enthusiasts, and sportsmen have only themselves to blame, for *The Last Stand* gives them a stern projection of what is to come.

July 1973
Washington, D.C.

Preface

Eyes drooping and fur falling out, Smokey the Bear spends his days lounging in the sun at the National Zoo in Washington, D.C. For twenty years, he and his Forest Service publicists have alerted the American people to the wild beauty of the National Forests and to the need to protect them from human destruction. "Only *you* can prevent forest fires," Smokey warned, and visitors to the National Forests heeded his warning.

Smokey symbolized the Forest Service of old. In his day, forest rangers cared more about building new campsites, stocking remote lakes with fish, and preventing the public from burning down its wilderness playground than they did about filling ever larger timber harvesting quotas. Forest Service officials approached their jobs with a sometimes arrogant professionalism, but also with a love and respect for the forest. With flair and energy, they worked to achieve "the greatest good of the greatest number in the long run."

In the last ten years, the spirit of Smokey has dissolved in the logging hysteria that grips the Forest Service. Pressured by the timber industry to speed the cutting of highly scenic timberlands in the National Forests, the Forest Service has been substituting a new respect for the timber dollar for its old respect for the land. Smokey continues to warn against forest fire, but the Forest Service has lost most of its rapport with the public.

Fortunately, the spirit of Smokey lives on in the actions of many Forest Service officials. A walk through the agency's architecturally stark headquarters in Washington, D.C., quickly convinces you of the fact. The electric, unbureaucratic atmosphere of self-confident professionalism, imagination, and dedication is startling. What the Forest Service needs is not new foresters, but new direction.

The National Zoo recently announced a bear cub successor to the aging Smokey. The Forest Service followed suit with the appointment of a new Chief—a personable, energetic, and highly qualified forester, John R. McGuire.

xix

We address this book especially to him and his Forest Service colleagues, not as a challenge to their authority, but as a hopeful appeal to their belief in the spirit of Smokey. Only *you,* guided by Congress and the public, can return the Forest Service to its noble aim of providing the greatest good from the National Forests to the greatest number in the long run.

Our Study Group of eleven lawyers, graduate students, and undergraduates began its examination of National Forest management policies (our investigation focused on the clash between timber production and nontimber uses of the National Forests; we did not analyze the major Forest Service functions of Forest Research and State and Private Forestry Cooperation) in the summer of 1970. Working primarily in Washington, D.C., we studied Forest Service files and other government and private materials, and spoke with dozens of Forest Service officials, members of Congress and their aides, White House personnel, timber industry executives, leading conservationists, and other persons inside and outside government. Thoroughly updating the information gathered by the Study Group, I wrote a preliminary draft report, which was released in December 1972 by the Center for Study of Responsive Law. In preparing the report for publication, I have rewritten much of it and again updated its findings. I am pleased to report that some of the updating was necessitated by welcome reforms in Forest Service policy.

We would like to thank the Forest Service for cooperating so fully with our study. Officials from the Chief on down gave generously of their time and answered promptly our many requests for information. The other persons with whom we communicated were also helpful.

Several Study Group members deserve special recognition. Henry Drummonds drafted parts of Chapters 2, 4, and 6, and suggested countless improvements in the entire text. Hale Andrews' perceptive essay on the Forest Service decision process provided case study material used in Chapters 2 and 4. Bonnie Temple helped bring project findings up to date.

I would personally like to thank several other individuals for their generous assistance. Harrison Wellford, Graham Allison, Mary Calfee, Peter Schuck, and Davitt McAteer offered helpful criticisms of the preliminary draft, and Henry Vaux graciously read part of the final version. Connie Jo Smith, Jeanne Dillon, and Ruth Fort expertly typed and produced the report, and Roger, Jane, and Jon Barney laboriously proofread it. Throughout the project, Rick Berkman gave needed encouragement and advice. Not to belittle the major contributions of others, I nonetheless take full responsibility for the contents of this book.

Daniel Rhodes Barney
Snowville, New Hampshire
July 1973

The Last Stand

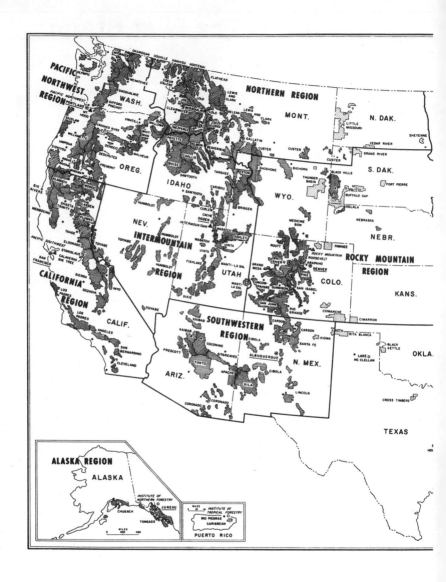

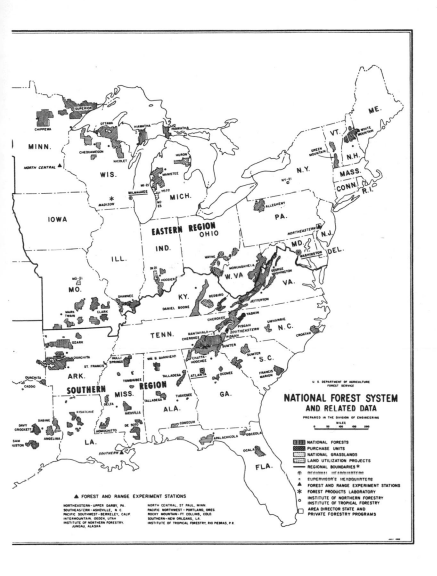

U. S. DEPARTMENT OF AGRICULTURE
FOREST SERVICE

NATIONAL FOREST SYSTEM
AND RELATED DATA

PREPARED IN THE DIVISION OF ENGINEERING

MILES
0   50   100   150   200

▨ NATIONAL FORESTS
▨ PURCHASE UNITS
▨ NATIONAL GRASSLANDS
▨ LAND UTILIZATION PROJECTS
— REGIONAL BOUNDARIES ✳
⊚ REGIONAL HEADQUARTERS
⊙ SUPERVISOR'S HEADQUARTERS
✳ FOREST AND RANGE EXPERIMENT STATIONS
△ FOREST PRODUCTS LABORATORY
○ INSTITUTE OF NORTHERN FORESTRY
INSTITUTE OF TROPICAL FORESTRY
☐ AREA DIRECTOR STATE AND
PRIVATE FORESTRY PROGRAMS

▲ FOREST AND RANGE EXPERIMENT STATIONS

NORTHEASTERN - UPPER DARBY, PA.
SOUTHEASTERN - ASHEVILLE, N. C.
PACIFIC SOUTHWEST - BERKELEY, CALIF.
INTERMOUNTAIN - OGDEN, UTAH
INSTITUTE OF NORTHERN FORESTRY,
JUNEAU, ALASKA

NORTH CENTRAL, ST. PAUL, MINN.
PACIFIC NORTHWEST - PORTLAND, OREG.
ROCKY MOUNTAIN - FT. COLLINS, COLO.
SOUTHERN - NEW ORLEANS, LA.
INSTITUTE OF TROPICAL FORESTRY, RIO PIEDRAS, P. R.

1   Gold in the National Forests

✢ ✢

> *What we are after is human happiness. Our problem then is to find how we may manage our forests so as to realize their highest potentialities for the well-being of mankind.*
>
> *This problem of management involves more than raising the maximum amount of timber. . . . We must recollect that it is possible for a forest program to lay too much emphasis on the forest itself and to consider insufficiently the related social values.*[1]
>
>   *Robert Marshall, then Director*
>   *of Recreation, Forest Service, 1933*

Early in 1964, the U.S. Forest Service unleashed an army of chain saws, logging tractors, bulldozers, and huge flatbed trucks on West Virginia's Monongahela National Forest. Their assignment then, and every year since, was to clearcut—remove every tree in one cut—large patches of the forest, and to haul the timber away to be made into lumber. And that, the Forest Service assured a dubious West Virgina citizenry, was the best means to a "desirable" end—boosting the Monongahela's timber yield.

Clearcutting, the Forest Service explained, was the first efficient step in a highly efficient scheme for producing timber, called "even-aged management." As in farming, you begin by clearing the land of brush and low-quality timber. Then you burn the entire area to dispose of the branches, stumps, and wood chips left after logging and scarify the site—scrape the earth bare with bulldozers—to prepare it for planting. Several years later, to protect the seedlings breaking through the soil from hungry animals and competing vegetation, you spray the area with pesticides and herbicides. Wait another forty years, and the new "crop"—of "even" age and uniform, high-quality species —is ready to harvest.

This scenario of economic efficiency did not impress the West Virginians living near Monongahela National Forest. It alarmed and angered them. For decades, they pointed out, the Forest Service had harvested trees and small groups of trees as they matured. This "selection" method enabled the agency to fulfill its obligation to manage the National Forests for "multiple use," including recreation, watershed, wildlife habitat, and range, as well as timber production. Many West Virginians had come to depend for their liveli- hood on serving the million tourists who annually visited the Monongahela Forest. To residents and tourists alike, the forest consisted, not of "low-quality timber," but of scenic hills and valleys full of majestic hardwood stands, clear streams, and abundant wildlife.

Who authorized the Forest Service to turn the Mononga- hela National Forest into a tree farm, the West Virginians demanded to know. And who authorized the Forest Service to apply a timber harvesting technique—clearcutting—that left the landscape looking as if it had been shelled and then napalmed, that reduced watershed and wildlife habitat, and that, through erosion and soil-nutrient depletion, threatened the long-run productivity of the forest's land and water? Led by the president of the Richwood Chamber of Commerce and a former Forest Service ranger, the West Virginians loudly protested the policy change to their state legislators and Congressmen.

Forest Service officials closed their ears to the growing outcry. Stubbornly they asserted that Forest Service re- search demonstrated that, without a doubt, clearcutting and intensified timber production were right for the Monon- gahela Forest. Exhibiting astounding independence, the Forest Service summarily dismissed the repeated com- plaints of West Virginia's U.S. Senators, Jennings Ran- dolph and Robert Byrd, two of the most influential men in Congress. It shrugged off a resolution passed by the West Virginia legislature calling for a moratorium on clear- cutting. And today, despite frequent protests from Senators Randolph and Byrd, the Forest Service continues to clear- cut blocks of the wild and beautiful forest.

Forest Service clearcutting has provoked similar protests in Alaska, Wyoming, Montana, and several other states. The practice has been hotly debated in numerous government and private studies, Congressional hearings, newspapers and books, and industry, professional and conservation group meetings (see Chapter 3). But public dissatisfaction with National Forest management extends far beyond clearcutting.

Mining in the National Forests, which involves at best the clearcutting and roading of large forest tracts and at worst the strip-mining of them as well, has led to numerous complaints. Late in 1972, the attorney general of West Virginia sued the Forest Service to limit destructive mining operations in Monongahela National Forest. Although hampered by insufficient funds, the Forest Service does police some thirty-two thousand mining claims, leases, and permits covering more than seventeen million acres of National Forest land. Recently the agency launched a research and demonstration project to reduce adverse environmental impacts of western strip-mining operations. But the Forest Service is powerless, under present mining laws, to block, or even strenuously regulate, the exercise of private rights to minerals underlying eastern National Forest land or the private appropriation of *any* National Forest land found to contain extractable minerals.[2]

The Forest Service has also been faulted for permitting too much livestock grazing on the 106 million acres of National Forest land open to that use. According to Earl D. Sandvig, a retired senior official of the Forest Service who has continued to monitor National Forest management in the West, "Overgrazing by domestic livestock and to some extent by game animals on our public lands is creating more soil erosion and denudation of land surfaces than all other uses put together."[3] Inadequate money for range management is partly to blame. So is the ability of powerful cattle growers' associations to outmaneuver the Forest Service. Farmers in Montana, Colorado, and Arizona who depend on a steady water flow from the National Forests to irrigate their crops have attacked the Forest Service for overgrazing.[4] Like clearcutting, it has caused water yields to fluctuate widely and the quality of irrigation water, fouled by soil and logging debris, to decline.

Condemnations of clearcutting have been accompanied by complaints about inadequate reforestation and improper road construction. The Forest Service theoretically assures reforestation of harvested sites in the National Forests through the Knutsen-Vandenberg ("K-V") Act of 1930.[5] The Act authorizes the Forest Service to require timber contractors to deposit, as part of the timber purchase price, funds for the reforestation of the area to be logged. Limitations in the Act, however, create serious funding difficulties. Potentially productive sites now stocked with low-quality timber frequently cost more to replant than the Forest Service gains from sale of the timber. Although the sale of valuable timber on other sites yields K-V deposits far in excess of the funds required to reforest them, the Act forbids the transfer of the extra funds to more needy sites. Finally, the Act provides little money for second attempts at reforestation when, as in ten percent of the cases, first efforts fail.[6]

Deficiencies in K-V funding and devastating fire, wind, insect, and disease attacks have created a "reforestation backlog" in the National Forests of almost 4.8 million acres —an area larger than Massachusetts. Each year, with direct Congressional appropriations, the Forest Service reforests a fraction of the backlog—100,000 to 150,000 acres —but new areas are cut down and little progress is made. The agency has proposed a ten-year, $315.6-million effort to replant about half of the backlog.[7] Thus far, however, Congress, and more so the President's Office of Management and Budget, have refused to provide the necessary funds.

National Forest visitors have also protested the erosion and water pollution resulting from improper construction of logging roads. Gouged out of hillsides and bottomlands by giant bulldozers, these roads lack durable surfacing and proper drainage. Intensive use by trucks and other heavy logging equipment in all kinds of weather can cause massive earth slides. Instances of such damage have been documented by the Forest Service in Georgia, California, Montana, and Wyoming.[8] Accordingly, in 1970, the Forest Service cooperated with the U.S. Environmental Protection Agency in the formulation of improved guidelines for road building.[9] Since then it has hired transportation consultants to review plans for expanding the 198,000-mile network of National Forest roads. It has also encouraged the development of logging systems requiring fewer roads, such as cable, helicopter, and balloon logging.[10] Nevertheless, according to a March 1973 review by the U.S. General Accounting Office—Congress's watchdog on the executive branch—environmental damage from Forest Service road projects continues. GAO attributed the problem to the agency's failure to "insure that the expertise of resource specialists was obtained and used to the extent practicable." [11]

Finally, nationwide Forest Service policies favoring timber production over nontimber uses of the National Forests have met with increasing public opposition (see Chapter 4). The agency's "environmental program"—a proposal to increase the timber yield of the National Forests by fifty percent within ten years—has led to allegations that the Forest Service pays too little attention to the impact of logging on the environment and nontimber uses.[12] The Forest Service's reluctance to preserve additional National Forest lands as wilderness has resulted in numerous lawsuits and the possibility of legislative intervention by Congress. The Forest Service budget, two-thirds of which funds items involving timber production, has given rise to complaints that the agency no longer manages the National Forests for *multiple* use.

Most of the dissatisfaction with Forest Service policies is reducible to a conflict between the timber industry and nontimber forest users over the level of timber harvesting in the National Forests (see Chapter 2). Executives of the multibillion-dollar industry are pressing for *more* timber cutting. They claim that the country needs more wood with which to build more houses, and that the National Forests can and must supply much of that need. In opposition, a growing segment of the public is demanding *less* cutting, to permit more nontimber use. Conservationists seek substantial additions to the 14.3 million acres of National Forest Wilderness and Primitive Areas already preserved from cutting; recreationists want more woodlands protected from cutting and more recreational facilities constructed to relieve present overcrowding in the National Forests. The Forest Service is caught in the middle.

Yet public concern over the devastating practices of the timber industry led to the creation of the National Forests in the first place. The industry had long followed a policy of "cutting and running" on privately owned timberlands.

It squandered America's rich timber resources and left behind a denuded landscape. Millions of acres of once productive forests were damaged by erosion and lack of reforestation. What enraged America's earliest conservationists, however, was the industry's subsequent assault on huge tracts of *public* forest land, obtained from the federal government by railroads and speculators.

The conservationists, led by John Muir, John Wesley Powell, Frederick Law Olmsted, and Gifford Pinchot, urged the government to save its timberlands from the private ax. In response, Congress authorized the President in 1891 to set aside portions of the dwindling public domain for protection as forest reserves.[13] Defying the land-grabbers and the loggers, Presidents Grover Cleveland, William McKinley, and Theodore Roosevelt quickly established reserves constituting most of the present National Forests west of the Great Plains. The Weeks Act of 1911 enabled the government to purchase lands, primarily in the East and South, for inclusion in the National Forest System.[14] Finally, the Land and Water Conservation Fund Act of 1965 established a fund for the purchase of new National Forest lands for recreation.[15]

Today the National Forest System encompasses 187 million acres—nearly a tenth of the land surface of the United States. Its 155 National Forests and nineteen National Grasslands average two thousand square miles each in area—roughly the size of Delaware. From Puerto Rico to Alaska, they span all kinds of climate, topography, and vegetation. In the Pacific Northwest they embrace some of the oldest and lushest woodlands in the country. They also include glaciers in Alaska, brush country in the Southwest, grasslands in the Great Plains, pine plantations in the South, and a tropical rain forest in Puerto Rico. Wildlife abounds everywhere.

The National Forests support a multitude of uses.[16] Eleven hundred watersheds, occupying forty million acres of National Forest land, provide water for most western and many eastern cities and towns. These watersheds also help irrigate twenty million acres of cropland and protect millions more from flooding. Over seven million head of domestic livestock graze on National Forest rangelands. Thousands of individuals and companies prospect for minerals, or mine them, in the National Forests. The Forest Service administers seventy thousand permits for "special uses"—television transmission sites, military installations, pipelines, airports, private homes and recreational facilities, and reservoirs. The forests also include wilderness and other protected areas of unique biological, geological, or scenic value.

The National Forests are used primarily, however, for recreation and timber production. In 1970, Americans spent 172.5 million visitor-days * in the National Forests— camping, hiking, hunting, fishing, swimming, skiing, snowmobiling, and sightseeing. In 1974, National Forest recreation use will soar to 198.2 million visitor-days, a 15-percent increase in four years, and more than double the use projected for the purely recreational National Parks.[17]

This trend reflects not only increasing population, mobility, and leisure time, but also growing recognition of the unique suitability of National Forest lands for many recreational activities. National Forest alpine areas, which contain many of the country's highest peaks, serve hikers and sightseers in the summer and skiers and snowmobilers in the winter. The eighty thousand miles of rivers and streams and the forty thousand lakes in the National Forests support an increasing demand for water sports and fishing. The abundance of game makes the National Forest System a hunter's paradise. Campers are allowed to hunt, fish, and gather firewood and forage in the National Forests, activities prohibited in the National Parks. In many parts of the country—particularly in the east—the National Forests are the only large natural areas open to the public.

The National Forest System's unique recreational treasure is 56 million acres of unroaded wild areas. Forests west of the Great Plains hold many of the remaining virgin stands—true wildernesses that have never been logged and are relatively untouched by man. They abound with majestic pines, redwoods, and Douglas-firs—yards in diameter, hundreds of feet tall, hundreds of years old. Beneath them flourish ancient, intricate plant and animal communities. Outdoorsmen maintain that there is a uniqueness about

* One visitor-day measures one person's use of public lands for recreation for twelve hours.

each of these wild areas which man could never replicate
if he were to cut down their mammoth trees.

But man is chopping them down. Although the standing
forests are valuable for recreation, they are also valuable
for the manufacture of lumber, plywood, paper, and other
wood products. Under Congressional authority, the Forest
Service cultivates, harvests, and regenerates National Forest timber. Following long-range management plans, it
auctions standing timber to private logging companies,
which harvest it under Forest Service supervision. In fiscal
year 1971, the National Forests yielded 10.3 billion board
feet of timber, or about 17 percent of the national harvest.[18]
Many of the virgin forests most appealing to recreationists
contain the most valuable timber stands left in the United
States.

Congress, by statute, and the Forest Service, by administrative action, have banned timber cutting on some old-
growth National Forest lands. But because they contain
the bulk of the National Forests' timber treasure, most of
them remain vulnerable to the chain saw and bulldozer.
The National Forests contain 217 billion cubic feet of wood
fiber—one-third of the nation's total.* They also contain
one-half of the nation's inventory of standing softwood
sawtimber—the high-quality timber used to build houses.
About one-fifth of the nation's commercial forest land † is
in the National Forests, and most of it contains old-growth
timber—mature trees, each with thousands of board feet
of potential lumber. For example, in the Douglas-fir supply
region of Oregon, Washington, and California—which em-
braces almost a quarter of the National Forests' inventory
of softwood sawtimber—seventy percent of the stands are
over ninety-five years old. Two-thirds of these are more
than 245 years old.[20]

To the timber industry, these old forests are "overmature." They are past the age of high growth rates and,
to a timber producer, cutting them down makes sense:

* See Appendix 1-1, "U.S. Timber Inventories, Removals, and Growth
(1970)."
† The Forest Service defines commercial forest land as forest land
which is producing or is capable of producing crops of industrial
wood and not withdrawn from timber utilization by statute or administrative regulation.[19] See Appendix 1-2, "Commercial Forest Land
Ownership."

young trees produce wood fiber at faster rates. "Forests are a renewable resource—a crop," industry lobbyists declare. To conservationists, the "crop" metaphor is grossly misleading. One can watch corn harvested in the autumn and see it standing full-grown in the field the next year; a Douglas-fir forest, however, takes the better part of a century to grow to harvesting size and centuries to grow to the sizes found in existing old-growth forests. Even if it is regrown, a forest, once cut down, is lost to generations. And the loss is not merely aesthetic, recreational, or ecological; it is also economic. During the decades it will take the new forest to reach maturity, society will be deprived of a regular supply of harvestable wood.

Largely to reconcile the demands of conservationists and loggers on the National Forests—which then, as now, were conflicting—Congress established the Forest Service in 1905.[21] To shield it from the land speculators and loggers who virtually ran the Interior Department, Congress placed the new agency in the Department of Agriculture. Since then, the Forest Service, with the help of friendly Congressional committees, has warded off numerous attempts by Presidents to transfer it to the Interior Department, which manages most of the federal domain. But the Forest Service is rapidly losing its autonomy through President Nixon's iron control over its budget, and Congress has proved unable, or at least unwilling, to thwart him (see Chapter 5).

To ensure the exercise of professional judgment unhampered by political pronouncements, Congress delegated to the Forest Service almost unlimited authority to manage the National Forests as it saw fit (see Chapter 5). During its first half century, the Forest Service functioned under the loose guidelines of the Organic Administration Act of 1897:

> No national forest shall be established except to improve and protect the forest within the boundaries for the purpose of securing favorable conditions of water flows, and to furnish a continuous supply of timber for the use and necessities of citizens of the United States.[22]

In 1960, at the request of the Forest Service itself, Congress elaborated the original guidelines, but still in broadly con-

struable language, in the Multiple Use–Sustained Yield
Act:

> It is the policy of the Congress that the national forests
> are established and shall be administered for outdoor
> recreation, range, timber, watershed, and wildlife and
> fish purposes. . . . The Secretary of Agriculture is
> . . . directed to develop and administer the renewable
> surface resources of the national forests for multiple
> use and sustained yield. . . . Due consideration shall
> be given to the relative values of the various resources
> in particular areas. . . . "Multiple use" means: the
> management of all the various renewable resources of
> the national forests so that they are utilized in the
> combination that will best meet the needs of the Amer-
> ican people.*

The Multiple Use Act, which merely codified long-stand-
ing Forest Service policy, is the creed of every Forest Service employee. Whenever an employee wants to attack a
land-use proposal, he declares it to be inconsistent with
multiple-use management. Whenever the agency as a
whole senses an external threat to its considerable autonomy, it shouts "foul!" and points to possible violations of
the Multiple Use Act. Its success at mediating forest use
conflicts by attacking its opponents as "dominant use"
extremists has won the Forest Service broad support in
Congress and with the public. And that support has enabled
it to exercise extraordinary discretion in the determination
of National Forest policy.

The concept of multiple-use management originated in
the Forest Service's initial mandate from the Secretary of
Agriculture. In a letter to the first Chief of the Forest Service, Gifford Pinchot (Pinchot himself drafted the letter),
Agriculture Secretary James Wilson directed:

> It must be clearly borne in mind that all land is to be
> devoted to its most productive use for the permanent
> good of the whole people and not for the temporary
> benefit of individuals or companies . . . and where
> conflicting interests may be reconciled, the question

* See Appendix 1-3, "Multiple Use–Sustained Yield Act of 1960."

will always be decided from the standpoint of the greatest good of the greatest number in the long run.*

Under Chief Pinchot and his immediate successors, the agency was crusading, even arrogant, in its advocacy of professional forestry and conservation. As Pinchot wrote in his autobiography:

> . . . every member of the Service realized that it was engaged in a great and necessary undertaking in which the whole future of their country was at stake. The Service had a clear understanding of where it was going, it was determined to get there, and it was never afraid to fight for what was right. . . .[23]

Though it has always been an agency that believed in material benefits from the forest as opposed to spiritual benefits (the first Forest Service manual was appropriately entitled the *Use Book*), the agency also inherited the Progressive Movement's desire for responsive government and efficient use of resources. It introduced new technology in growing trees and coping with forest fires and pests, and castigated its private forest land opponents for not following suit.

As the Service aged, its domain grew larger with the addition of several million acres of forest land in the East. The agency initiated research and private forestry assistance programs. During the Great Depression, it sponsored one of the most innovative and constructive efforts of the New Deal: the Civilian Conservation Corps. Employing thousands of jobless citizens, the Corps reforested huge tracts of land devastated by dust storms, forest fires, and excessive timber cutting. Later the Forest Service launched programs in international forestry assistance. It also established public recreation areas and restricted wild areas, many of which have since become National Forest Wilderness Areas.

Today, the agency's chief function is the protection and management of the 187-million-acre National Forest System.† Its activities include constructing and operating recreational facilities and administering permits for ski de-

* See Appendix 1-4, "Policy Directive."
† See Appendix 1-5.

velopments and other special uses of the National Forests. The Forest Service also sells tracts of National Forest timber to private logging companies, supervises the cutting, and reforests the harvested areas. In addition, the agency manages watersheds, rangelands, and special wildlife habitat areas. Protection of the National Forests involves fire prevention and suppression as well as insect and disease control. Management policies are formulated in the sparsely staffed office of the Chief of the Forest Service in Washington, D.C. They are implemented by a field organization of 9 regional foresters, 129 forest supervisors, 774 forest rangers, and thousands of auxiliary personnel.

The Forest Service carries on two other major functions: forest research and state and private forestry cooperation. Nearly a thousand Forest Service scientists conduct research to improve the management, protection, and utilization of forest resources throughout the country. They work in eight Forest and Range Experiment Stations, a Forest Products Laboratory, and seventy other research forests and installations. Cooperative forestry activities involve supplying limited technical and financial assistance to the state and private owners of 574 million acres of forest land.*

The Forest Service employs approximately thirty thousand men and women, mostly in the field. On the whole, it has managed to attract some extraordinarily competent employees. More decentralized than most federal agencies, it has believed that "the job is on the ground," and for many years it did a widely acclaimed job on the ground. It has been justifiably proud of its competence and professionalism.

But, as one Forest Service official put it, "Multiple use is like Christianity: easier to preach than to practice." [24] In the last five years, the Forest Service has come under increasing fire for its management policies. In this report, we will examine some of these policies: their formulation and implementation, and their impact both on National Forest users and on the forests themselves.

---

* Because our investigation focused on the conflict between timber production and nontimber uses in National Forests management, we will not discuss in detail the Forest Service functions of research and cooperative forestry.

2

✿ ✿

The Conflicting Legacies
of Paul Bunyan and
Henry David Thoreau

If you'll permit me to suggest it, we need to get the National Forest timber show back under the big top. It seems we're so busy attending sideshows where the attractions are—really distractions—arguments about wilderness, timber harvesting methods, single use vs. multiple use, ad infinitum—that we forget what Congress said were the purposes of the National Forests more than 76 years ago. Among other things, those were ". . . securing favorable conditions of water flows and to furnish a continuous supply of timber for the use and necessities of citizens of the United States. . . ."[1]
  W. D. Hagenstein
  Industrial Forestry Association, 1973.

In a realistic and practical sense, what is in the National Forests represents literally the very last opportunity for preservation and protection of these parts of our national heritage while there is still time. Our forests also contain some of the finest opportunities to observe or to hunt and fish for wildlife. . . . Unfortunately, the policy of the Forest Service towards these values—particularly the value of wilderness—seems to have been one of maximum exploitation of other resources, with the overwhelming emphasis on timber.[2]
  Brock Evans
  Sierra Club, 1971.

17

The timber industry unwittingly provoked today's sharp controversy when, a decade ago, it began lobbying for the acceleration of timber production in the National Forests. Bending to the pressure, the Forest Service introduced large-scale clearcutting, postponed reforestation, logged vast wildernesses, and downgraded recreation, watershed, wildlife habitat, and other nontimber forest uses. Meanwhile, the American population rapidly grew, as did the amount of their leisure time and their interest in the natural environment. Public-private skirmishes over the proper use of the National Forests were inevitable.

Today, undaunted by growing public opposition, the timber industry is pressing for still more timber cutting in the National Forests. Its publicized rationale is pure altruism: downtrodden city-dwellers, seeking new homes, will not get them, or be able to afford them, without a boost in National Forest timber output. As we shall see, the real reason for the industry campaign—a multimillion-dollar effort organized on the hustings and in Washington by a powerful lobby—is unadorned profit-seeking. Having squandered the once vast reservoir of private timber, the industry now needs federal timber to keep its mills operating.

Other users of the National Forests lack the timber industry's organizational muscle and leverage in Congress. Nevertheless, individually and in groups, they are vigorously contesting the industry's proposals. If the Forest Service expands the National Forest timber harvest, they warn, it will be liquidating a recreation and wildlife resource—much of it wilderness—which Americans need now more than ever and which can never be replaced. They argue that if the country needs more wood with which to build more houses, it should look to other sources. Increased recycling of paper and wood products, reduced wood waste in the harvesting and processing of timber, and expanded timber production from nonindustry private laws could greatly augment existing wood supplies.

Historically, America's private forests have supplied the bulk of its timber needs. Up to World War II, the National Forests, which encompass most public timberlands, provided less than five percent of the national harvest.[3] "The political pressure was to preserve the old-growth timber on National Forest lands," Murl W. Storms, Chief of Forestry at the Bureau of Land Management, explains. "Harvesting it would have lowered stumpage [raw timber] prices on private lands." [4] Aside from the timber industry's desire to keep prices high, private timber production has predominated because private timberlands are more extensive, more productive, and at one time contained more standing timber than public timberlands.

Almost three-quarters of the 499.7 million acres of commercial forest land in the United States are privately owned.* The forest products industry owns 67.3 million acres, and some four million farmers, outdoorsmen and other individuals and nontimber companies own the remaining 296.2 million acres. The National Forests include 91.9 million of the 136.1 million acres of public timberlands; the rest belongs to a score of federal agencies and state and local governments.

Second, the potential productivity of most private forest lands exceeds that of most public forest lands. Forest Service analyst Robert W. Larson recently calculated the potential net annual growth per acre of forest lands under different ownerships in the North, the South, the Pacific Coast area, and the Rocky Mountains. In every region, forest industry lands turned out considerably more productive than National Forest lands. In three regions—the North, the South, and the Pacific Coast—nonindustry private lands also proved more productive than National Forest lands. [5]

Originally, too, private lands held more timber than public lands. In 1953, private forest lands contained 53 percent of the country's standing sawtimber, the valuable timber cut from large trees for lumber and plywood. Public lands contained only 47 percent. But two hundred years of "cutting and running" by the timber industry have severely depleted the private sawtimber inventory. Today it is the public lands that contain 53 percent of the country's standing sawtimber, and the private lands that contain 47 percent. [6]

With the drop in private timber inventory, the annual yield of private forest lands has markedly declined. Since national timber demand has risen steadily since 1920 while supply has remained more or less constant, the Forest

* See Appendix 1-2, "Commercial Forest Land Ownership."

Service has been under increasing pressure to take up the slack left by private producers with an expansion of National Forest timber cutting. Accordingly, though fewer National Forest acres are devoted to timbering (93.1 million acres in 1952; 91.9 million in 1970), the National Forests provided 8 percent of the national harvest in 1952, and twice that throughout the 1960's.[7]

The Outlook for Timber in the United States, a comprehensive Forest Service study released in 1972, predicted that the decreasing timberland base and growing concern for nontimber forest values will necessitate a leveling off of National Forest timber output in the coming decades.[8] But timber shortages, presaged by continued industry cutting of private lands at rates exceeding annual growth, could create political pressures capable of changing the Forest Service's mind.

Several Forest Service reports document the alarming trend in private timber cutting. The 1969 *Douglas-fir Supply Study* predicted that continued cutting at current rates on the private old-growth forests of western Oregon and Washington and northern California "would lead to a 65 percent reduction in annual private harvests within 30 years. . . ." The report noted that in 1933 there was more than twice as much private timber as National Forest timber in the Douglas-fir region. By 1963, however, less than half of the timber remaining in this area stood on private lands.[9]

A 1970 Forest Service report identified the same pattern in California, the third-ranking state in timber production. Despite rising demand, log production in California dropped 11 percent between 1955 and 1968. "The privately held old-growth reserves of Douglas-fir . . . have been rapidly depleted," the report observed, and public timberlands have been called upon to make up the difference:

> The moderate decline in California's log production in recent years tends to mask the decreasing availability of private timber. During the period 1955–1968, total log production in the state decreased 11 percent, but log production on private lands decreased 43 percent. During the same period, log production from public lands—primarily National Forests—increased 240 percent, making up for most of the decline in private log production.

The depletion of private timber and the tremendous pressure to cut extensively on public lands have resulted from a sizable excess of cut over growth. "In 1965," the Forest Service report stated, "sawtimber harvest was double the sawtimber growth in California."

Excessive timber cutting in California will continue into the next century. In 1980, the Forest Service report revealed, cut will still exceed growth by 46 percent, and in the year 2020, by 25 percent. Consequently, California will suffer a 28-percent decrease by the year 2020 in its inventory of standing sawtimber. The reduced inventory, in turn, will lead to a simultaneous 20-percent decline in the state's annual timber harvest.[10]

The Forest Service's 1972 *Outlook* report offers some hope for a reversal of private cutting trends. Despite a projected decrease in the output of timber industry lands, nationwide production of softwood sawtimber is expected to exceed its 1970 level by 4 percent in 1980 and by 13 percent in 2020.[11] But these expectations are based on the presumption—of questionable validity—that the timber yield of nonindustry private lands will soar over the next fifty years. Recently these lands have produced timber in amounts disproportionately small considering their large area and potentially high productivity. As we will show later, neither industry nor government appears willing to make the heavy investments in improved forestry needed to stimulate the timber yield of these lands.

The industry's excessive cutting policies are partly an outgrowth of the "cut out and get out" philosophy that earlier guided its destructive sweep across the continent. Although it has repudiated the philosophy, its primary interest in connection with public and nonindustry private lands remains, understandably, the removal of timber—not its regrowth or the protection of nontimber forest uses. At the 1973 meeting of the Southern Forest Institute, an official of the huge Weyerhaeuser Company readily admitted that the industry still overcuts the private lands that it does not own:

> The ultimate blame for overcutting or poor cutting on private lands lies with our industry. Forest products on private lands are cut by contractors and through wood dealers who supply us. Thus, indirectly, we are responsible for cutting practices.[12]

But the industry is also overcutting its own old-growth timberlands. It justifies the practice on the ground that rapid replacement of "overmature" timber with fast-growing young trees will eventually permit a sustained annual yield exceeding today's. In the intervening decades, however, the nation is deprived of an even flow of high-quality, old-growth timber, and logging communities are deprived of a steady source of jobs. Continued harvesting of industry lands at present levels could plunge much of the rural Pacific northwest into economic depression. Forest Service studies project that by 1980 over one-quarter of Eugene, Oregon's forest products employment in 1963—and forest products employment constitutes 71 percent of the city's basic employment—will be wiped out. The same fate will befall Eureka, California, which is equally dependent on the lumber industry. Worst of all, relief may not come for generations: a Douglas-fir forest takes decades to regenerate.[13]

Most industry lands—which in 1970 produced 28 percent of the nation's timber harvest—are owned by major seedling-to-stationery manufacturing concerns. Industry leaders in 1972 were International Paper (7.0 million acres, $2.09 billion in sales), Champion International (2.0 million acres, $1.87 billion in sales), Georgia-Pacific (4.5 million acres, $1.77 billion in sales), and Weyerhaeuser (5.6 million acres, $1.68 billion in sales). But the top twenty-one companies account for only ten percent of total industry sales. Almost 52,700 smaller companies are responsible for the remainder.[14] Lacking extensive lands of their own, the smaller firms depend for raw material chiefly on public and nonindustry private lands. In 1970, these ownerships accounted for 24 percent and 48 percent, respectively, of the nation's timber output.[15]

As a whole, the timber industry is an economic giant—the country's seventh largest industry. Its sales of $43 billion in 1971 constituted 5.7 percent of total U.S. sales of $751 billion. Its 1,636,000 employees—about the same number as in the food industry—made up 8.5 percent of the country's manufacturing labor force.[16]

MAKING FRIENDS IN HIGH PLACES

The timber industry's importance in the economies of some cities and states gives it political leverage over a number of Congressmen. In Oregon, for example, it employs 47.7

percent of all manufacturing workers, with a payroll of $613.6 million. In Washington, the corresponding figures are 23.2 percent and $490.7 million. In highly industrialized California, the forest products industry annually pays $906.1 million to 122,000 workers—7.5 percent of the state's manufacturing labor force. In most of the other states leading in timber production—Georgia, Alabama, Louisiana, Mississippi, North Carolina, Virginia, Florida, Maine, Tennessee, and Idaho—the timber industry's share of manufacturing employment exceeds 10 percent.[17] Many cities and counties in forest regions are even more dependent on the timber industry. In Portland, Oregon (population 382,600), 16 percent of total employment involves wood harvesting or processing; in Humboldt County, California (population 105,000), over 40 percent is timber-connected; and in Roseburg, Oregon (population 14,500), 80 percent.[18]

The rapid depletion of private timber resources could cause massive unemployment in these areas within the next ten or twenty years. Timber industry jobs are already being eliminated rapidly by technology. According to the Forest Service, increasing labor productivity alone will cause timber industry employment to shrink 14 percent from its 1963 level by 1980.[19]

Lost jobs can mean lost votes. Senators and Congressmen from major timber producing states, therefore, have tended to respond favorably to the industry's push for more National Forest timber cutting. The National Timber Supply Act of 1970, an industry-initiated bill to expand the National Forest timber harvest, received the active support of all six Oregon and Idaho Congressmen and the four Washington and two California Congressmen representing major timber producing districts. The measure nevertheless failed in the full House by a vote of 228–150.[20]

In 1968, then Senator Wayne Morse of Oregon chaired Senate hearings into timber supply shortages and proposed a successful amendment to the foreign aid bill of that year limiting the export of raw timber from federal lands. In so doing, according to Wendell Barnes, then head of the Western Wood Products Association, Morse "successfully answered" the timber industry's "request." The industry had lobbied for the amendment partly to prevent Japanese importers from destroying its lucrative monopoly on the processing of federal timber.[21] In 1973, Morse's successor, Senator Bob Packwood, introduced legislation banning the export of timber from federal lands immediately and from all nonfederal lands by July 1, 1976.[22]

Oregon's senior U.S. Senator, Mark O. Hatfield, has likewise championed the timber industry's cause. In 1971 he introduced a bill similar to the ill-fated National Timber Supply Act to spur timber production in the National Forests.[23] The Senate Subcommittee on Public Lands, on which Hatfield sits, held hearings on the bill but, in the face of Forest Service opposition,[24] the full Senate Interior Committee has yet to report out any major timber legislation.

Timber states are powerfully represented on the Congressional committees that process forestry legislation. Senator Henry M. Jackson (Democrat of Washington) and Representative James A. Haley (Democrat of Florida)— from the second- and sixteenth-largest timber producing states, respectively—chair the Senate and the House Interior Committees. The chairmen of the Senate and the House Agriculture Committees, Senator Herman E. Talmadge (Democrat of Georgia) and Representative W. R. Poage (Democrat of Texas), represent the fourth- and fourteenth-ranking states. And Senator John L. McClellan of Arkansas, the ninth-largest timber producing state, and Representative Julia Butler Hansen (Democrat of Washington), respectively, head the full Senate Appropriations Committee and the House Appropriations subcommittee that handles the Forest Service budget.[25]

Senators and Congressmen from timber states tend to keep in close touch with the industry. Representative John Dellenback (Republican of Oregon), who represents Oregon's heavily timbered Fourth Congressional District, used to employ a former official of the timber lobby as his administrative assistant.[26] George C. Cheek, executive vice-president of the timber industry's American Forest Institute, spent six months in 1968, before coming to AFI, working full-time for the reelection of influential Senator Warren G. Magnuson (Democrat of Washington).[27]

Most of these legislators and others in a position to further timber interests have received campaign contributions from the industry's Forest Products Political Education Committee (FPPEC).[28] FPPEC's total 1970 campaign contributions of $26,394 are dwarfed by COPE's (AFL-CIO)

$969,328 and AMPAC's (American Medical Association) $693,413, but the committee is eager to catch up. In 1970, FPPEC circulated among its patron companies a chart contrasting its small contributions—most were in the $200–$1000 range—with those of other groups. At the bottom, in prominent lettering, was printed: "The need for increased forest products industry support is obvious!" [29]

To supplement its political efforts at the local level, the timber industry has developed an impressive national lobbying and public relations operation. The National Forest Products Association (NFPA) and the American Forest Institute represent most industry interests in Washington, D.C. NFPA, a federation of twenty-two regional, species, and wood-product trade associations, grew out of the old National Association of Lumber Manufacturers. Headquartered in the new redwood-paneled Forest Industries Building on Massachusetts Avenue, NFPA lobbies for new laws, bigger appropriations, and more action by the Forest Service to swell the flow of National Forest timber to industry sawmills. It also pressures key members of Congress, the White House, and the Forest Service to "protect the national timber base from excessive withdrawals for non-timber use." Its $1-million budget, supported by dues from member associations, finances public relations and the wide distribution of economic and technical forestry information as well as lobbying. "The staff maintains personal contacts with more than thirty agencies and departments," a recent NFPA brochure claims.[80]

Interactions between NFPA and the Forest Service are frequent, and relations generally good. The Chief of the Forest Service often makes speeches at the conferences of NFPA and its member associations. Many industry foresters received their start in the Forest Service. Through meetings of the professional Society of American Foresters and informal contacts, they keep in touch with their former colleagues. Charles Connaughton, after retiring in 1971 as a Forest Service regional forester, became a vice-president of NFPA's largest member group, the Western Wood Products Association.

SELLING THE "GREAT AMERICAN FOREST"

Stung by the conservationists' victory in the National Timber Supply Act fight, the industry decided in 1970 to

upgrade its public image. "We have little time left to act,"
one logging executive warned a 1972 convention of his
fellows. "The critics are gaining on us every day, saturating
the public mind with ridicule and criticism of our industry." [31] The American Forest Institute, with offices several floors beneath NFPA in the Forest Industries Building,
was assigned the task and George C. Cheek, an aggressive
but personable advertising executive and onetime logger,
was hired as its new director. With several hundred thousand dollars collected from timber companies, Cheek
launched a drive to convince the public to stop worrying
about the effect of timber harvesting on the environment
and to begin worrying about an impending shortage of
wood. Cheek placed full-page, full-color advertisements in
large-circulation magazines, sought promotional assistance
from the leaders of other industries, and visited radio and
television talk shows to publicize the industry's new environmental concern.

AFI has concentrated its efforts on reaching the public
indirectly, by cultivating more sympathetic treatment of
the timber industry in the national media. Last year, for
instance, AFI's advertising agency designed a dramatic,
eighteen-page booklet called *Forests USA*, which appeared
as an insert in *Editor & Publisher* magazine. Sporting
photo-montages of lush forests and gleaming wood products, the booklet tries to persuade the reader simultaneously
that the nation ought to be chopping down more trees and
that the timber industry really is concerned about protecting the forest environment for recreation and wildlife
habitat.

Forests USA was distributed to thirty thousand news
executives through *Editor & Publisher*. A half million
copies have reached the general public through newspaper
inserts and timber company distribution. AFI, together with
the Southern Forest Institute, has also been pushing for
more favorable coverage of the industry in the press by
conducting forest tours for editors and news executives.
Cheek is now considering extending the tours to other
"opinion-makers," including doctors, lawyers, and government officials.

A Gallup poll conducted in April 1972 for the Forest
Industries Council—the industry's policy-making body—
indicated the extent of the public's ill feelings toward the

industry.[32] A majority of those interviewed thought that "taking into account both the need for lumber and paper and the need to conserve our timberlands, there is too little emphasis on conservation." A majority also believed that "the forests are being used up faster than trees can be grown as a result of timber cutting by lumber and paper companies." More than three-quarters of those interviewed considered clearcutting "a bad practice." Three out of every five people interviewed said that the government should control the way lumber companies use their own forests.

Two months after completion of the poll, FIC ordered AFI to extend and intensify its public relations effort. It voted to provide AFI with $4.25 million through December 1974. Half of this amount, assessed from member companies at thirty cents per $1,000 in 1971 sales, will be devoted to advertising.[33]

The accelerated campaign reflects a new FIC belief that "the industry needs to *inform* in a straight-forward manner before it can effectively *persuade*." Accordingly, AFI advertisements in national magazines as well as diverse trade and professional journals have attempted to dispel the widely held notion that timber cutting is eating away at the "Great American Forest." Displaying a color-coded map of the country's forested areas, one ad proclaims:

> The great American forest is closer than you think. Wherever you are. . . . Much of the forest has been harvested and regrown three or four times. And, public or private, government or individually owned, much of it is available for hunting and fishing, picnicking and camping . . . It's right there in your backyard, keeping America green—and growing.[34]

Objective and innocent enough on its face, the ad is nonetheless a vehicle of subtle persuasion, not information. True, the country still has an abundance of forest *land*. True, much of it is in "your backyard," available for public recreation. But the Great American *Forest*—the wild, unmanipulated domain of the two-hundred-year-old Douglas-fir, the jumbled glade of oaks and birches, and the clear, free-flowing stream—is every day shoved farther away by industry chain saws. The "forest" to which the AFI ad refers is less and less a natural forest. It is fast becoming one big pine plantation, whose clearcuts and row-after-row of identical tree "stems" will hardly appeal to the ad's readers as a desirable place for "picnicking and camping." But, from the industry's viewpoint, what the public does not see—and few members of the largely urban American public have seen a regimented industry tree farm—will not hurt it.

RATIONALIZING A RAID ON
THE NATIONAL FORESTS

With a self-caused decline in private timber harvests fast approaching, industry leaders in the mid-1960s trained their sights on the huge timber resources of the National Forests. Appealing to Congressmen from timber producing areas and lobbying with Congressional committees and White House staffers, they began pushing the Forest Service to accelerate National Forest timber cutting. The Forest Service acknowledged the growing pressure in its 1966 budget message to Congress:

> This [fiscal year 1967] program increment reflects the increasing dependence industry is placing upon National Forests to supply their roundwood requirements. It is also indicative of industry pressure to expand its raw material sources into heretofore inaccessible and lower quality timber. There are pressures in the timber resources management program that are becoming increasingly difficult to contain.[35]

This minor increase in funding and National Forest timber yield was far less than the industry had in mind, but in 1966 it lacked a rationale capable of persuading Congress to respond more vigorously to its demands. Two years later, skyrocketing lumber prices provided the necessary justification—spurious, but nonetheless convincing to a Congress jarred to attention by general inflation in the economy. The National Association of Home Builders, meeting in Washington in late 1968, enthusiastically agreed to join NFPA in the fight for more National Forest timber cutting.[36]

Over the next year and a half, they pushed in vain for Congressional passage of the National Timber Supply Act (see Chapter 4). Presupposing the support of most western Congressmen and Republicans, the lobbyists concentrated on the eastern, big-city liberals, arguing that:

(1) only a leveling off of lumber prices would permit construction of the millions of cheap homes urgently needed by city-dwellers;

(2) only an increase in raw timber supply could halt rising lumber prices; and

(3) only the National Forests could furnish the increase in raw timber.

In March 1973, rising lumber prices triggered another combined industry assault on the executive and legislative branches to obtain large increases in National Forest timber output. Appealing to the sympathetic Senate Housing Subcommittee with the same three-point rationale as in 1969, NFPA spokesmen argued that "the timber management functions of the Forest Service must be much more greatly emphasized." The subcommittee, whose chairman, John Sparkman of Alabama, has often championed timber causes, quickly approved legislation to accelerate National Forest timber production—almost a carbon copy of the 1969 bill. At this writing, environmental groups are successfully mustering Congressional and citizen opposition to the legislation.

Eager for immediate government action, the industry lobbyists began knocking on doors in the Executive Office Building as well. One week after 2,125 homebuilders and lumber dealers convened in Washington to demand increased federal cutting, the President's Cost of Living Council directed the Forest Service to expand greatly the volume of timber it planned to sell in 1973. The directives from Washington came amidst unprecedented reductions in Forest Service personnel ordered by the President's Office of Management and Budget. With many Forest Service field officers openly apprehensive about their ability to produce increased timber yields without causing serious ecological harm, Secretary of Agriculture Earl Butz sent the Regional Foresters a terse memorandum commanding them and their subordinates to keep quiet publicly about their misgivings. In June 1973, the Natural Resources Defense Council, the Sierra Club, the Wilderness Society, and other national environmental groups sued the Forest Service to enjoin it from increasing timber harvesting until it prepares an environmental impact statement on the action. Due to the lawsuit, the Forest Service's own coldness to the increase, and, ironically, the sizable drop in lumber prices since spring 1973—which could deter logging companies from purchasing the extra timber to be put up for sale—the Forest Service may never get around to executing the sales increase.[37]

However cogent, politically, the industry's justification may have sounded in 1969 and 1973, it was bunk, economically. The price of a new home varies chiefly with the cost of construction labor, land, and financing—not lumber. According to government statistics, lumber accounts for only 17 percent of the construction cost, and only 9 percent of the fully financed cost, of the average single-family dwelling. It makes up an even smaller percentage of the cost of most multifamily dwellings.[38] Consequently, without accompanying restraints on the other important cost factors, measures to dampen lumber inflation can do little to hold down the price of new homes. As Eugene Gulledge, Assistant Secretary of Housing and Urban Development, pointed out at hearings before the Senate Subcommittee on Public Lands in June 1971, "factors other than lumber may very well have a greater inflationary impact on housing costs." In particular, he cited construction industry wages and the prices of land and financing, both of which "have been increasing more rapidly than prices of most other goods and services." [39]

Moreover, since the rise in lumber prices was not caused mainly by an insufficient raw timber supply, an increase in that supply could not by itself have halted the price rises. Lumber prices soared in 1968–1969 principally because of a shortage of *lumber*, not a shortage of *timber*. The lumber shortage resulted from problems in the conveyance of wood products from the harvesters to the lumber retailers. These problems included rising log exports to Japan, a dock strike impeding importation of logs, a shortage of railroad boxcars slowing domestic timber flow, and the attempts of many retailers who, gambling on lower wholesale prices, had kept inventories down, only to be caught by rising demand.[40]

The timber industry's contention that only an increase in timber harvest could ease the retail price situation was pure political expedience. If it had really been concerned about short-term raw timber shortages, it could have begun harvesting the huge volume of uncut National Forest timber which it had already purchased—over two years' worth.[41] But, according to NFPA economist John Muench, Jr., the industry recognized in the lumber inflation crisis a golden opportunity to obtain a permanent expansion of National Forest timber sales: "Since the determination of National Forest cutting levels is a political decision, we needed the proper political climate to push for an easing of supply constraints. That climate was present in 1968." [42]

ALTERNATIVE SOURCES OF WOOD

Finally, the industry's contention that only the National Forests could furnish needed increases in raw timber ignored the existence of alternative sources of additional wood. These include importing more timber, making fuller use of the domestic wood now harvested, recycling more paper and other wood products, and, most important, expanding the timber yield of nonindustry private lands.

As U.S. wood consumption has risen over the last half century, this country has become increasingly dependent upon the timber resources of other countries. Wood imports, principally from Canada and the tropics, reached 2.7 billion *cubic* * feet in 1971—one-fifth of the wood consumed by the United States in that year.[43] U.S. wood exports, primarily to Japan, have also been rising, approaching 1.2 billion cubic feet in 1971. The 1.5-billion-cubic-foot import surplus that year accounted for 12 percent of total U.S. wood supply.

Some change in the import/export ratio is expected in the coming decades. According to the Forest Service, expanded timber production in Canada, Southeast Asia, Africa, and Latin America could boost U.S. wood imports to 4.7 billion cubic feet by the year 2000. Although U.S. wood exports are expected to reach 2.6 billion cubic feet in 2000, ongoing State Department negotiations with Japan—which purchases 85 percent of the wood now exported—could re-

* The volume of usable wood fiber ("roundwood") obtainable from a given tree or forest is measured in *cubic* feet. The amount of processed lumber obtainable from a given tree or forest is measured in *board* feet (12 inches x 12 inches x 1 inch). Because some wood volume is lost in manufacturing lumber from round logs, the smaller and more irregular the tree, the lower will be its ratio of board feet to cubic feet. Timber volume statistics are a layman's nightmare, especially because the Forest Service, until recently, measured all volumes in board feet (allowable cut, although described in board feet, is still used to measure total roundwood volume).

duce that figure. Assuming no such reduction, the net import balance will nonetheless rise from 1.6 billion cubic feet in 1971 to 2.1 billion in 2000. In the long run, of course, dwindling timber resources in timber-surplus countries could severely reduce U.S. imports. For substantial, long-term increases in timber supply, the United States will have to depend on domestic measures.

Making fuller use of timber now harvested could immediately augment wood supply. In 1970, over 1.6 billion cubic feet of slash and small or dead trees were left to rot on logging sites. Sawmills burned or discarded an additional one billion cubic feet of wood residues, and secondary manufacturing plants wasted another 800 million cubic feet. Most of the two billion cubic feet of bark removed at sawmills was also discarded. The timber industry already makes profitable use of some residues not included in the 4.4 billion cubic feet just described. And the Forest Service estimates that prospective improvements in technology will lead to a 4-percent-per-decade increase in the "product output" of a given volume of raw timber. The agency's 1972 *Outlook for Timber in the United States* identified a number of opportunities for making fuller use of existing wood supplies, including:

—modifying timber sale practices "to encourage and force more complete use of wood materials now wasted"; *

—accelerating the development and adoption of new processing technology in lumber and plywood manufacture, such as the use of thinner saws;

—developing particle boards, manufactured from sawdust, bark, and other residues, as substitutes for plywood;

—improving the construction design of houses and other structures to reduce wood requirements (without increasing nonwood material requirements);

—developing methods of timber harvesting which would minimize adverse environmental impacts so as

* In mid-1973, the Forest Service promulgated a new regulation directing its field officials to include in all future timber sales contracts "as appropriate such requirements as to provide . . . (f) Complete utilization of the timber as may be attained with available technology." [44]

to make timber production feasible on areas where it
is now uneconomic or environmentally unacceptable;
—improving the means of providing advice in the
adoption of new technology.

Realization of these goals will require investments in research far greater than either industry or Congress and the
President have been willing thus far to make.

The Forest Service report also urged the stimulated development of wastepaper recycling technology. Wastepaper
has long supplemented pulpwood as a fiber source. Two
decades ago, 31 percent of the fibrous material used in
paper manufacture was wastepaper. Today, the availability
of cheap pulpwood and the lack of economical methods for
large-scale recycling have reduced wastepaper use to about
19 percent of total fibers. But, as the Forest Service has
observed, "Increasing concern over pollution of the environment, and the growing costs and difficulties of solid waste
disposal, have stimulated much interest and action by Government and industry to increase recycling." As a result,
the Forest Service reports, use of wastepaper will rise to
22 percent of total fibrous materials used by 1980, and to
34 percent by the year 2000.[45]

Public opposition to the accelerated cutting of the
country's forests, necessitated by soaring lumber and plywood consumption, could force the paper industry to boost
the recycling rate even sooner. The National Academy of
Sciences has concluded that to satisfy paper needs double
those of today and to cope with worsening solid-waste
problems, the United States will have to recycle 35 percent
of its annual paper consumption by 1985.[46] The Bank of
America, the country's largest bank, asserted in a December
1971 report that this rate was attainable: "Our own research indicates that this goal is technologically feasible
and—theoretically at least—is economically feasible, too."[47]
Japan and several western European countries already recycle 25 percent or more of their wastepaper.[48]

The manufacture of paper and related products now
consumes nearly *half* of all timber harvested in the United
States. Therefore, almost any increase in recycling would
permit a larger proportion of the timber now harvested to
be manufactured into lumber and plywood needed for resi-

dential construction. It would also relieve some of the pressure for increased cutting in the National Forests.

The best hope for expanding domestic timber supply— and the most difficult to realize—is to improve the management of the millions of acres of potentially productive forest lands in nonindustry private ownership. These lands today furnish about one-half of the country's annual timber yield. If managed more intensively, they could supply a far greater portion, and thus reduce the urgency of expanding timber production in the National Forests.

Four million farmers, city-dwellers, and other individuals and nontimber companies own three-fifths of the nation's 500 million acres of commercial forest land. According to the Forest Service, many of these lands are potentially as productive, measured by climate, accessibility, and soil, as industry lands that were purchased specifically for their ability to produce timber.[49] Nevertheless only 5 percent of these vast, fertile lands are intensively managed for timber production. A third of the nonindustry private lands are managed for eventual harvest, but with limited and usually unplanned forestry techniques. Nearly half of the owners of the lands display no interest in intensified forestry, although from time to time they sell timber grown by nature. The remaining 15 percent of the lands are held for nontimber purposes, including developmental speculation as well as recreation.[50]

The Forest Service concludes from ownership studies that "most forest owners do not consider timber growing investments to be sufficiently profitable to take priority over other investment or consumption opportunities." [51] The answer, it declared—echoing many professional foresters, industry executives, and conservationists—is to *make* intensified timber management profitable through a vigorous program of public and private, technical and financial assistance.

The Forest Service and numerous state agencies for years have extended purely technical assistance to small private owners. In 1971, some 1600 government foresters spent $24.1 million offering advice to forest owners. The Forest Service also provides over $20 million annually to the states for fire protection and forest tree planting on private lands.[52] Neither the Forest Service nor state agencies, however, furnish private owners with direct cost-sharing assistance. Not surprisingly, government aid programs have reached few forest owners and resulted in no appreciable increase in nonindustry private timber yield.

Although the Forest Service denies it is proposing a cost-sharing program, its 1972 *Outlook* report describes and justifies in detail two such possible programs. In one case, Forest Service researchers identified 9 million acres on which a ten-year program of intensified reforestation, stand improvement, and commercial thinning to boost softwood sawtimber yield would return more than five percent on the additional costs of accelerated regrowth. They also identified 8.1 million acres of nonindustry private land in the southeastern United States where intensified management to increase the yield of all varieties of timber would return an equal amount on investment. The former program was estimated to cost $346 million; the latter, $724 million.[53]

Although the Forest Service report notes that "a major share of this cost was assumed to be Federal," the Nixon administration apparently thinks otherwise.[54] In 1972, its opposition to Congressional legislation establishing a pilot cost-sharing program contributed to its death in House committee. Ignoring Forest Service skepticism evident in the Senate hearings,[55] the Administration declared that any such program should be left up to the states, which could, if they wished, finance it out of the President's proposed revenue-sharing fund for community development.[56] The Senate, which passed the bill regardless, apparently shared the view of many foresters that the states, even with revenue-sharing, would be far less able, or willing, to assist private forest owners than the federal government.

Two additional ways to improve the timber management of private lands, not yet considered by the Forest Service or Congress, deserve study. First, a program of legal and financial incentives to encourage *timber industry* investment in improved management of small private lands might prove less costly to taxpayers and more effective in the long run than a direct federal subsidy program. In 1969, a far-thinking industry group, the Southern Forest Resource Analysis Committee, proposed a massive public-private effort to triple the annual timber yield of southern forests by the year 2000. The projected yield of 15.7 billion cubic feet would exceed the current timber output of the entire country by a third, and at the turn of the century could supply much of the nation's timber needs.[57] In its report, *The South's Third Forest*, the committee outlined its plan, which focused on the small private forest owner:

> The owner could dedicate his land to forest production and pay some fraction of the development cost. The Federal Government could continue to pay a share of the cost of planting, timber stand improvement, or other practice through ACP [Agricultural Conservation Program]. The Forest Service could continue to provide cooperative funds through State Foresters to plan, supervise, and check compliance. Forest industry could then, perhaps, justify an agreement to provide annual payments to the owner of developing timberland for a future supply of wood. With an immediate income in prospect, many more landowners might take the initiative and request funds and services.[58]

While accepting the report's recommendations, the industry has scarcely begun to implement them.[59]

An alternative to both industry and government cost-sharing is federal purchase and intensified management of selected productive forest lands now in nonindustry private ownership. The Forest Service has never seriously considered this idea because, according to Associate Chief Rexford A. Resler,

> It generally would not be economically or socially feasible for the Federal Government to purchase large acreages of private lands of the kind that would be included in a forestry incentives program. The average Federal cost per acre for stimulating the practices studied in the 1970 Timber Review was $32. The kinds of lands involved in such practices would sell for much higher prices than $32 per acre.[60]

Associate Chief Resler errs in comparing only the immediate costs and not the long-term costs and benefits of purchase as opposed to subsidization. The average taxpayer stands to recover little from a forestry incentive program which doles out thirty-two dollars per acre to small private owners. The expansion of timber yield from this investment will not come for years, and when it does, it will not appreciably alter wood product prices. Tax revenues on the expanded yield may eventually assist some timber communities but will scarcely benefit *national* taxpayers— whose interests every federal program supposedly serves first.

Federal purchase and intensified management would admittedly require a greater initial outlay. In the South, where many of the most productive private forest lands lie, recently cut timberland is selling at about one hundred dollars per acre.[61] Timber companies, buying selectively and in large, discounted tracts, have often paid less. Moreover, the very fact that these companies *are* buying timberland—five million acres nationwide in the last ten years [62]—and not just leasing it or purchasing timber rights on it, would seem to contradict Associate Chief Resler's contention that federal purchase, if followed by long-term intensive management, would not be "economically feasible."

Federal purchase and management would not only provide taxpayers the 7- to 8-percent return on investment now enjoyed by industry timberland owners in the South.[63] It would also add to the public lands now open to recreation and other nontimber uses (although these lands, unlike the National Forests, would presumably be managed chiefly for timber). The federal government would, of course, have to condemn and purchase selectively, paying attention to the special needs of local communities and individual owners. In particular, to avoid the inequities caused by present purchases for the National Forest System (see Chapter 5), the government would have to compensate communities for reductions in property tax revenues. But these are minor obstacles, easily overcome.

It is difficult to understand the reluctance of the Forest Service or the Congress to consider the purchase alternative. The reason cannot be lack of precedent. Most of the 23.2 million acres of National Forest land east of the Great Plains were acquired through purchase, and more are being bought each year. The National Park Service and the Forest Service have purchased more than a million acres of private land—much of it forested—for recreation since passage of the Land and Water Conservation Fund Act of 1965.[64] And the Bureau of Reclamation and the Army Corps of Engineers have been purchasing land for vast reservoirs throughout this century. Nevertheless, federal subsidy programs are so popular with Congress that, unless blocked by the President, it will probably enact one in the forestry field before it even considers the land purchasing alternative.

COUNTERVAILING RECREATIONAL NEEDS

In the decades before private timberland production once again assumes major proportions, the timber industry would like to see the liquidation of the National Forests' reserves of big timber. Only this drastic action, it argues, can keep Americans supplied with cheap new homes. Besides, it says, the forests are "renewable."

This logic has an appealing simplicity, but only because it sidesteps the main issue with which Congress must grapple. The public clearly has an interest both in maintaining an adequate supply of reasonably priced housing and in conserving the unique treasures of the National Forests for wilderness, recreation, wildlife habitat, watershed, and range, as well as timber production.

Although the timber industry is loath to admit it, Americans are clamoring not only for cheap new homes, but also for more open space and facilities for outdoor recreation. In the words of one National Park Service official, "The American public has an insatiable appetite for recreation." [65] An increasing population, a rising standard of living, and a growing interest in the natural environment will whet the public's appetite in the coming decades. Forty years ago, a renowned Director of Recreation for the Forest Service, Robert A. Marshall, suggested an additional reason for the trend:

> As society becomes more and more mechanized, it will be more and more difficult for many people to stand the nervous strain, the high pressure, and the drabness of their lives. To escape these abominations, constantly growing numbers will seek the primitive for the finest features of life.[66]

According to a survey by the Bureau of Outdoor Recreation, participation by Americans in outdoor recreation will increase from 6.8 billion occasions in 1965 to 10.1 billion in 1980—a 56-percent rise. Participation will soar to 16.8 billion occasions in the year 2000—a 160-percent increase over 1960. Many of the recreation activities in which participation will increase by 150 percent or more—including walking for pleasure, swimming, sightseeing, boating, camping, and hiking—frequently involve use of forested public recreation areas.[67]

The National Parks will accommodate some of this increased participation. According to the Park Service, the Parks will receive 243.7 million visits * in 1975 and 302.8 million in 1981—increases of 21.5 and 51.0 percent, respectively, over use in 1971.[68] Some of the increased recreational demand will involve greater use of lands and waters managed by the Army Corps of Engineers, the Bureau of Land Management, and the Bureau of Sport Fisheries and Wildlife. State parks will also be used more.

By far the most intense pressure for expansion of recreational capacity, however, will be applied to the National Forests. Already, under the enlightened recreation management of the Forest Service, they sustain each year almost as many visitor-days of recreation use as the National Parks and the BLM and Army Corps lands combined.† In recent years, visitation has been increasing by four to six percent annually. Recreation use of the National Forests was 172.5 million visitor-days in 1970. By Forest Service estimate, it will increase to 198.2 million in 1974 and 250.6 million in 1980.[70] The National Forests will receive the bulk of the increase in recreational participation, quite simply because they are the only lands outside the relatively small National Park System that are both suitable and available for large-scale public recreation.

If the National Forests are to satisfy America's spiraling reaction needs, large portions of them will have to be saved from the ravages of timber production. Logging is always ugly and is frequently destructive of the forest environment. When clearcutting is used, the uprooting of trees, the scarring of the land by heavy logging equipment, and the burning of slash leave harvested areas looking like bomb sites. Even selection cutting—the removal of single trees or groups of trees—significantly detracts from the

* *Visits* are entries into areas and facilities managed by the National Park Service—not stays of a fixed duration. *Visitor-days*—which the Park Service records in much smaller numbers (see below) are recreation visits of twelve hours each.

† In 1969, the National Forests received 162.8 million visitor-days of recreation use, the National Parks, 66.4 million, the lands managed by the BLM, 38.8 million, and the Army Corps, 72.1 million.[69]

aesthetic and recreational value of the forest. Damage caused by timber cutting may persist until the forest has thoroughly regenerated itself—twenty-five, fifty, or a hundred years after harvesting. Many of the National Forests' ancient stands of fir, pine, and redwood are aesthetic and ecological masterworks that man can never replace, no matter how "intensive" his management of them.

Notwithstanding industry rhetoric, the public's interest in maintaining an adequate, reasonably priced housing supply can be served without leveling the old-growth National Forests. All that is required, in addition to stimulating wood supply in the ways already suggested, is vigorous governmental control of rising land, financing, and construction costs, and a rationalizing of the present subsidization of new home purchasing.

The federal government already subsidizes the purchase of new homes indirectly through National Forest timber operations. Because of their relatively low productivity, the harvesting, regrowth, and second harvesting of many National Forest lands entail dollar costs far exceeding returns. When the costs (not always measurable) of avoiding and mitigating damage to the environment and to opportunities for nontimber use are figured in, the excess of costs over benefits applies to most, if not all, National Forest lands under timber management.

Under such circumstances, managing these lands for timber production keeps nationwide lumber prices artificially low at the expense of the taxpayer and the forest environment. Moreover, most of this subsidy ends up in the pockets of logging companies, lumber dealers, and home builders. Very little, in the light of the small proportion of home construction costs attributable to lumber, trickles down to the home buyer.

The American public, through its elected representatives, may well deem it to be in the national interest to subsidize the purchase of new homes. If so, the subsidy should come not out of the uneconomic, environmentally destructive logging of the National Forests, but out of general federal revenues—collected by income tax from those best able to pay. And the subsidy should go directly to those home *buyers* who need financial assistance.

3

**Clearcutting: Technology
and Turmoil**

*The [Forest] Service has been slow and in-
sensitive to the awakening national awareness
of our environment. Until recently, it has failed
to perceive the shocking impact of clearcutting
devastation on the public senses. It has continued to view clearcutting through purely professional blinders as one of the best ways to
grow and harvest timber given certain conditions. It has failed to understand that clearcutting should be judged not only as a timber
harvest device, but also with respect to its
environmental impact. . . .*[1]

                    Edward C. Crafts
                    Former Deputy Chief of the
                    Forest Service, 1972

I. The Public on the Rampage

To achieve the expanded timber output demanded by lobbyists and some elected officials, the Forest Service in the
mid-1960s sanctioned extensive clearcutting in the National Forests. The ugly results of clearcutting—the removal in one cut of all the trees on a site—infuriated
National Forest users from Georgia to Oregon.

Residents of communities adjacent to clearcuts were
especially distressed. "The Forest Service is knocking down
and burying and burning the next 150 years of future in
our area," a Darby, Montana, logger complained in mid-
1969. "They're destroying our forest and our livelihood."
Clearcutting on the Bitterroot National Forest was removing so much timber so fast that "pretty soon there won't
be any more to log." [2] Brock Evans, Washington, D.C., representative of the Sierra Club, flew over recent clearcuts on
the Bitterroot and reported: "Logging like you see in the

41

Bitterroot isn't logging, it's mining. . . . The Forest Service is extracting a resource in a way that essentially de-
stroys that resource." Evans compared the cutover hillsides
to strip-mined areas, in both appearance and susceptibility
to erosion. The Bitterroot's terrain, he said, was too fragile
to support extensive logging and roading.[3] G. M. Brandborg, supervisor of the Bitterroot National Forest from 1935
until his retirement from the Forest Service twenty years
later, told a reporter in 1969:

> Forestry practices today are entirely different from
> those applied when I was associated with the Forest
> Service. I am positively astounded over the scarring,
> tearing up of the landscape, destruction of reproduc-
> tion and young trees well on their way to provide the
> next crop of timber. Erosion, destructive effects of
> burning undisposed slash are very much in evidence.
> Seemingly, foresters have lost feeling for the good
> earth.[4]

But clearcutting of a cruder sort predated Brandborg's
tenure as Bitterroot supervisor and even the establishment
of the Bitterroot Forest. It arrived with the earliest white
settlers. To make room for farms and villages, they gradually clearcut much of the virgin forest along the East Coast.
Before long, the rising demand for wood with which to
build cities and ships and to fuel homes and industries gave
rise to the American timber industry.

First with the ax, then with the saw, and eventually with
huge mechanized equipment, the industry clearcut its way
across the United States. It started in Maine, swept through
New York and Pennsylvania, and by the 1890s had de-
voured much of the white pine wilderness of the old Northwest Territories. Finally, as the juggernaut penetrated the
redwood and Douglas-fir kingdom of the Far West and the
pine forests of the South, a few lonely voices—John Wesley
Powell, John Muir, and Frederick Law Olmsted among
them—bitterly protested the ravaging of the North American forest. It sickened them that the loggers could "cut and
run" with impunity, never pausing long enough after clearcutting to reforest the denuded landscape.

The conservationists, growing in numbers during the
Populist era, coalesced around Gifford Pinchot, who was
later to become the first Chief of the Forest Service. By
1891 they had persuaded Congress and President Grover

Cleveland to withdraw large portions of the public domain and designate them as "forest reserves," safe from industry clearcutters. These became the first National Forests. In 1905, they were placed under the stewardship of the Forest Service, established that year by Congress, largely through the efforts of Pinchot's close friend, President Theodore Roosevelt. For decades Forest Service officials regularly condemned clearcutting. Then, in the early 1960s, the Forest Service reversed itself and began clearcutting heavily, especially in the west. Its foresters now claimed that clearcutting could be justified as a means of increasing timber production and growth—when applied properly and followed by reforestation measures.

Clearcutting, its current proponents argue, enables the forester to create "even-aged" forests of desirable tree species which will be capable of producing crop after crop of valuable timber. Such "intensive forest management" is necessary, they claim, because nature rarely "maximizes" timber yield and growth on its own. To "convert" natural forests to even-aged management—in the absence of strong environmental or nontimber forest use constraints—the forester usually clearcuts the old forest. Clearcutting is cheap, and it provides the most complete preparation for manipulated regrowth.

But clearcutting is not the only way to create an even-aged forest. The forester may also prescribe shelterwood or seed-tree cutting. The shelterwood method removes all merchantable timber from an area in two or three cuts. At the same time, it leaves behind enough trees to provide shelter from wind and sun for the natural reproduction of the forest. The seed-tree method, a variation of the shelterwood method, leaves behind just enough trees of desired species to seed the harvested area. After a few years, the shelterwood or seed trees are removed. Both methods leave the harvested site looking at least partially like a living forest.

A forester not intent exclusively on maximizing timber yield and growth frequently practices far less drastic uneven-aged management. Seeking to preserve the integrity of the existing forest while securing from it both timber and nontimber benefits, he can choose from two cutting methods: individual tree selection and group selection. The first involves the periodic removal of single mature trees;

Overlooking a recently clearcut, terraced area in Mud Creek
Drainage on the West Fork Area, Bitterroot National Forest,
Montana. *U.S. Forest Service photo.*

Shelterwood cutting, an example in the Pacific Northwest. Enough trees have been harvested so that shade-intolerant Douglas-fir will regenerate itself, but enough trees have been left to provide a source and to protect seedlings from frost, which frequently is fatal to young seedlings. Logging residue has not yet been treated. After treatment and seedling establishment, the shelterwood trees will be removed. *U.S. Forest Service photo.*

Group cutting in a California forest consisting of groups of trees of different ages and species (pine and true fir).

Stand left after a random selection experimental cutting on Piquett Creek Experimental Area, Bitterroot National Forest, Montana. *U.S. Forest Service photo.*

the second, the removal of groups of trees on sites a fraction of an acre to several acres in size. The surrounding forest takes care of reforestation, occasionally with the help of some planting or seeding.

Clearcutting accounts for much of the evident deterioration of the National Forests. Its extensive application by the Forest Service—in fiscal years 1970 and 1971 the Forest Service clearcut almost one million acres of National Forest land [5]—triggered the current debate over management of the forests. The clearcutting crisis in the Bitterroot National Forest had been simmering for several years when Dale A. Burk, a reporter for the Missoula, Montana, *Missoulian,* publicized it in 1969. A year before, large-scale Forest Service clearcutting and unsuccessful attempts at reforestation had led many Bitterroot Valley residents to complain to agency officials, state legislators, and members of Congress. Hoping to contain and resolve the controversy as a unique local problem, the leaders of the Forest Service reacted slowly to the public outcry. Finally, in May 1969, Regional Forester Neal Rahm appointed an agency task force to make an "impartial and penetrating analysis of management practices on the Bitterroot National Forest." In December 1969, U.S. Senator Lee Metcalf (Democrat of Montana) asked the University of Montana School of Forestry to study the controversy.

The Forest Service task force reported to Rahm in April 1970. It supported many of the citizens' complaints: "The Task Force agrees that scenic quality has been substantially impaired in many places at the very least for a period of years." The report continued:

> The Task Force believes . . . that clearcutting has been overused in recent years. In many cases, esthetics has received too little consideration. It is apparent to us that a preoccupation with timber management objectives—all the way from meeting allowable cut goals to efficient establishment of regeneration—has resulted in clearcutting and planting on some areas that could have been partially cut.[6]

The Select Committee of the University of Montana, chaired by Forestry School Dean Arnold Bolle, came to a similar conclusion in its November 1970 report: "Multiple use management, in fact, does not exist as the governing principle on the Bitterroot National Forest." Agreeing with many of the Forest Service task force's observations, the Bolle Committee report added: "While the rate and methods of cutting and regeneration can be defended on a purely technical basis, they are difficult to defend on either environmental or long-run economic grounds." [7]

Release of the Forest Service and Bolle Committee reports brought little affirmative action by the Forest Service. Finally, on July 26, 1971, Regional Forester Steve Yurich (who had replaced Rahm) directed Bitterroot Forest supervisor Orville Daniels to implement the recommendations of the Forest Service task force.[8] Since then, Daniels has significantly altered management practices, reducing the application of clearcutting from 61 percent of the annual timber harvest to 25 percent.[9] The new multiple use management plans being prepared for each of twenty-eight watershed planning units in the forest exhibit, for the most part, a new sensitivity for environmental values and public use preferences. Brandborg, Burk, and their fellow critics are taking a wait-and-see attitude in hopes that on-the-ground management practices will catch up with the new planning attitude.[10]

As noted in Chapter 1, clearcutting on West Virginia's Monongahela National Forest sparked a similar controversy several years ago. Hundreds of West Virginians have protested the clearcutting, which they see as a threat not only to the beauty of their forest land, but to their livelihoods as well. Many West Virginians earn their living serving the one million tourists who visit Monongahela National Forest every year.

The critics have garnered the support of professional foresters and economists, past and present Forest Service personnel, the state legislature, and West Virginia's powerful U.S. Senators Jennings Randolph and Robert C. Byrd.[11] But to no avail. Again and again the Forest Service has affirmed its application of even-aged management and clearcutting to the Monongahela National Forest. Senator Randolph reported in December 1972:

> Although the U.S. Forest Service has stated its policy has changed in Eastern Hardwood Forests—including the Monongahela National Forest—there is no evidence to suggest that even-aged management does not remain as the policy on the general forest zone [82 percent of the Monongahela's total area].

And the Senator warned, "Until this policy does change, there shall be no lessening of the continuing controversy." [12]

In May 1973, the Izaak Walton League and several other national conservation groups brought suit to enjoin the Forest Service from clearcutting the Monongahela. They argued that statutes limit timber harvesting on the National Forests to "dead, matured, or large growth of trees" and require that timber, before being sold, be "marked and designated." Both provisions are generally violated with clearcutting, which involves removal of all trees, from healthy saplings to diseased giants, and no individual marking of trees to be cut. As of this writing, the judge had not ruled on the suit. [13]

Forest Service clearcutting in the Wyoming National Forests has denuded large swaths of the Rocky Mountain countryside; some of these areas remain unforested and severely eroded a decade after cutting. After surveying these lands in 1969, U.S. Senator Gale W. McGee (Democrat of Wyoming) told his Senate colleagues:

> I visited areas in the Bridger [National Forest] region, one of which had been clearcut, as I remember, in 1957 or 1958, and which then, 11 years later, looked like a B-52 had devastated it. The land was gutted out. Huge mounds of earth were piled up with an odd assortment of trash timber. Regrowth was negligible to put it in liberal terms. What grabbed me on this was that we are not even talking about my kids going back there to enjoy that area, and probably not even their kids. [14]

The Forest Service confirmed his observations in its own 1971 investigative report on the Wyoming National Forests:

> We believe that public concern about over-harvesting is an understandable reaction to visible evidence on the ground. . . . There was some evident damage to wildlife habitat and to soil stability. More frequently, a potential for such damage was clear, although no evidence of damage could be found. Damage to the scenic quality of the landscape, however, was unmistakable. [15]

Neither Forest Service clearcutting nor the public uproar surrounding it have been restricted to the highly publicized cases of Wyoming, West Virginia, and Montana. Public censure of the practice is widespread. Dozens of incredulous, angry citizens from all over the country traveled to Washington, D.C., in April 1971 to testify against National Forest clearcutting before the U.S. Senate Subcommittee on Public Lands.[16] Dozens more protested the practice at subcommittee field hearings in Atlanta, Georgia, Portland, Oregon, and Syracuse, New York.[17] And the subcommittee announced in March 1972 that it had received "thousands of letters from throughout the Nation expressing interest in the future of our forests." [18] Since release of the preliminary draft of this study group report, we have received complaints from National Forest users concerning Forest Service clearcutting in Colorado, Oregon, Georgia, and Maine.

Public concern over clearcutting extends beyond its application in the National Forests. Many witnesses testifying at the Senate subcommittee hearings decried the clearcutting disasters they had encountered on forest lands owned by the timber industry, particularly on lands adjacent to National Parks and National Forests.[19] U.S. Senator Lee Metcalf and U.S. Representative John D. Dingell (Democrat of Michigan) responded to this criticism by introducing in the last Congress a bill to regulate private forest management practices.[20]

In October 1972, the Northern Environmental Council, which represents citizens' groups in Michigan, Wisconsin, Minnesota, and the Dakotas, published a critique of clearcutting as it is applied in North Central forests. Its authors, all professional foresters, urged the Forest Service, the timber industry, and small private landowners to switch from clearcutting to a biologically safer, more conservative array of cutting methods.[21] An editorial in the February 1973 issue of *American Forests* magazine referred to the council's paper in warning that the small woodland owner —the owner of 59 percent of the nation's forest land, upon whom the nation will one day depend for most of its wood supply—"doesn't care much for clear-cut logging and he tells AFA [American Forestry Association] he wouldn't be above locking up his woodlot until both the industry and bureaucracy get over their extreme clear-cut notions." [22]

II. Clearcutting: Why the Uproar?

The sources of the clearcutting controversy are largely those of the broader National Forest debate. In the face of growing public criticism, the forestry profession, and the Forest Service in particular—proud of its widely acclaimed record of wise forest management—has bitterly resisted the layman's encroachment on its field of expertise. In this resistance the Forest Service has been bolstered by the timber industry, which has exerted enormous pressure, via the White House and key Congressmen, on the Forest Service to increase the timber yield of the National Forests. Bigger yields are often obtained through more intensive cutting—in other words, clearcutting. At the same time the Forest Service, along with most of the forestry profession, has come under the spell of advancing technology and applied it without sufficient prior consideration of its impact on the natural environment. Moreover, the new timber technology has generated a view of the forest as nothing more than a reservoir of natural resources to be exploited, albeit wisely. Until quite recently, this view had nearly displaced the once prevalent understanding of the forest as an ecology constituting a valuable part of man's environment.

ENTRENCH AND RESIST

Perhaps the most obvious and consistent feature of the local conflicts over clearcutting has been the Forest Service's intransigence when confronted with citizen's demands for a reassessment of National Forest management practices. In Montana and West Virginia, Forest Service officials initially ignored public outcries. When the West Virginia critics picked up Congressional support, the officials took note of their allegations, but only long enough to dismiss them as biologically unsubstantiated. At the height of the Monongahela National Forest controversy, Forest Supervisor Frederick A. Dorrell confidently tutored an angry U.S. Senator:

> Research and experience have clearly demonstrated that the even-aged management system, which includes clearcutting, is the best way to manage our forest's timber stands. We, therefore, do not intend to depart from even-aged management as the basic tim-

ber management system on the Monongahela National Forest.[23]

Today, despite continuing complaints from citizens' groups, professional foresters, and West Virginia's Congressional delegation, the Forest Service has held fast.

When it finally got around to investigating the Montanans' complaints, the Forest Service did acknowledge its blunders and did make substantial improvements in the management of the Bitterroot National Forest. But the change of heart came only after a Forest Service review team had verified the citizens' allegations. The team reported that "communications with the public and other interested agencies have been seriously inadequate. . . . Full opportunity must be provided the interested public to express its views on policy and program matters *as they are being developed rather than after the fact*" (emphasis added.) [24]

In more recent clearcutting skirmishes elsewhere around the country, some Forest Service officials have shrugged off criticism with the same blind self-assurance which proved fatal in Montana and West Virginia. Nevertheless, despite its continuing reluctance to admit the public into the substantive stages of decision-making, the Forest Service has made admirable attempts to improve National Forest management. Five agency review teams in the last three years turned up evidence corroborating many of the protesters' charges. To a large extent, Forest Service leaders have since endorsed the teams' findings and directed local management personnel to carry out their recommendations.

The review teams urged reforms primarily in multiple use planning, location and design of timber cuts, and communication with the public. None of the teams, however, suggested severe limitations on even-aged management or clearcutting—the concepts most at issue in the public protests. On the contrary, they enthusiastically endorsed the practices. The Chief's Special Review Committee on the Monongahela National Forest declared in its report, June 3, 1970:

> There is no question that even-aged management, correctly applied, provides an orderly and beneficial system for regulating timber production. . . .

> Why then the controversy? Why the public concern?
> Why the need to appoint this Committee? Not because
> of the even-aged management system. The system is
> not on trial. On trial is the manner in which this sys-
> tem has been applied.[25]

For the protesting citizens of West Virginia, the system
was and still is on trial. L. W. Deitz, a member of the West
Virginia Forest Management Practices Commission, wrote
in mid-1972:

> The Forest Service has responded by making a great
> many minor changes such as smaller clear cuts; but
> they still adhere to the use of even-aged management
> and clear cutting on the general forest zone. This is
> entirely unacceptable in the eastern mixed hardwoods
> when we consider the many variables involved. This
> opinion has been expressed by a great many profes-
> sionals.[26]

And U.S. Senator Jennings Randolph of West Virginia has
since confirmed Deitz's observations.[27]

With public concern mounting, the Forest Service
launched in late 1970 a nationwide review of National
Forest timber management. Following an initial survey, the
agency released on March 26, 1971, a report identifying
thirty problem situations requiring action.[28] On June 14,
1972, it published an *Action Plan* to deal with them.[29]
Problem number one was "to increase Forest Service sensitivity to esthetic values in planning and executing timber
harvest, road construction, and site preparation." To solve
it, the Forest Service announced it would soon begin:

> (1) training Forest Service personnel of all disciplines
> to recognize esthetic values and incorporate them into
> their everyday work, (2) planning functional activi-
> ties so that the land is managed with due considera-
> tion of its esthetic qualities, and (3) establishing
> guidelines which protect the esthetic resource while
> the above efforts are becoming fully effective.[30]

Another important problem was "to recognize those areas
where timber will not be harvested because there is no
suitable alternative to clearcutting and environmental impacts make clearcutting unacceptable." The *Action Plan*
proposed "identifying on the ground those areas on which
environmental impacts are such that clearcutting is unac-

ceptable." The Forest Service would then direct that on those areas "the timber will not be harvested until such time as it can be accomplished without unacceptable environmental impact." [31] For each of the thirty problem situations, the *Action Plan* announced which officials would implement the proposed actions and which would hold the former accountable. It also established deadlines for accomplishing the reforms.

This vigorous, comprehensive effort represents a remarkable departure from previous Forest Service thinking. But to what extent the change in attitude will lead to changes in on-the-ground practices remains unclear. The nationwide review will exclude clearcutting from some fragile and scenic areas. It will also blunt the visual impact of clearcutting where it is practiced. Like the local reviews which preceded it, however, the report has glossed over the fundamental conflict between clearcutting and the nontimber uses of the National Forests protected by statute. Unaware of, or unwilling to acknowledge, the conflict, the Forest Service has given no consideration in the nationwide review to replacing clearcutting with individual and group selection cutting. Both selection methods would eliminate many multiple use conflicts by protecting nontimber uses during timber harvesting. Group selection cutting—the harvesting of mature trees in small groups—in particular, deserves further study. Initial research suggests that it could both satisfy the economic and biological demands of efficient timber production and preserve the forest environment for nontimber uses.

Nevertheless, the *Action Plan* outlined significant management reforms. Whether or not they will result in improved conditions on the National Forests depends on the cooperation of local agency officials. The mixed results of a recent reform effort on Montana's Bitterroot National Forest constitute a discouraging case in point. Following an inspection of the forest last June, newspaper correspondent Dale A. Burk reported that "some of the old problems are still occurring, though not as common as before. The main problem still seems to be that the rangers are not maintaining adequate surveillance of logging operations on their districts." Burk thinks the Regional Forester Steve Yurich's wide-ranging policy reforms are not being fully implemented because Bitterroot supervisor Orville Daniels

> has not reprimanded or evidenced any firm measures
> of control to his people on the ground to hold them
> accountable for what they do. . . . I fear that the re-
> sult of Daniels' unwillingness to get tough with his
> people is that the achievement of the quality level of
> management Yurich wants will be delayed or, in some
> cases, not achieved at all.[32]

Since the *Action Plan*'s directives resemble Regional Forester Yurich's, their implementation may be similarly de-
layed by resistant Forest Service field personnel throughout
the country.

The *Action Plan* ignores the conflict between clearcutting
and nontimber uses partly because the Forest Service
avoided public involvement in formulating it. If the Forest
Service had consulted the individuals and groups whose
protests had prompted the nationwide review, it would
have been forced to consider the use-conflict issue. But it
kept the review internal and asked for Congressional and
public comments only *after* release first of the "problem
situations" report and then of the *Action Plan*.

History goes far in explaining the Forest Service's resistance to public participation in its substantive decision-
making. Congress originally endowed the Forest Service
with considerable independence expressly to shield its forestry "experts" from the political and economic pressures
which previously had led to the devastation of some public
domain and much private forest land. Today, with the public leveling charges of mismanagement at the Forest Service as well as at private landowners, the Forest Service has
taken full advantage of its independence. While recognizing the need for more public participation, it has reserved
to its own professionals all National Forest management
decisions. A consultant to the Forest Service reported in
September 1972 that:

> Some Forest Supervisors showed [in interviews] a de-
> sire to seek advice from the public as to priorities in
> the initial stages of the investigatory process, as in
> the formulation of District or Forest level multiple use
> plans. Others, however, felt that agency expertise
> should be dominant in the policy formulation process,
> and the public consulted primarily for informa-
> tion. . . .

The public, if the numerous articles in the news media are indicative, prefers the former approach, allowing local residents actual involvement in decisionmaking.[33]

The Forest Service recently established guidelines for its field officials which should result in greater substantive public involvement.[34] In considering how best to protect de facto wilderness areas in eastern National Forests, the Service conducted numerous public "listening sessions" around the East, and some field officials have provided opportunities for public involvement early in the formulation of new forest multiple-use plans. And whenever officials have filed Environmental Impact Statements as required by the National Environmental Policy Act,[35] the officials have conformed to the law by soliciting public comment.

Nevertheless, numerous lawsuits brought by conservation groups attest to the Forest Service's reluctance to file Environmental Impact Statements and to allow sufficient public involvement in the making of many far-reaching land management decisions.[36] In the absence of a clear legal mandate requiring it to involve the public in decision-making, the Forest Service has often done no more than provide after-the-fact information on its decisions. As Elizabeth Peelle of the Oak Ridge National Laboratory's Environmental Program observes, "Real, though limited, efforts to involve the public in early stages of land use planning have been made since 1970, *but no formal public rights in questioning, advising, or initiating forest management policy exist*" (emphasis added).[37] Until such rights are created, the Forest Service can look forward to continuing public protest.

PRESSURES FROM ABOVE

The second element common to both the clearcutting controversy and the National Forest debate is the effect on Forest Service decision-making of the timber industry's drive to increase National Forest timber production. Funneled through the White House and Congress to the office of the Forest Service Chief and thence down the chain of command, this pressure to increase the timber harvest has led some field officials to clearcut excessively and abusively.

In partial defense of the erring supervisor of the Bitterroot National Forest, a Forest Service study team noted acidly:

> The emphasis on resource production goals is not unique to the Bitterroot National Forest and does not originate at the National Forest level. It is the result of rather subtle pressures and attitudes coming from above. *While the goals of management on the National Forests are broad and sound, the most insistent pressure recently has been to increase the timber cut* on these National Forests in order to make more timber available to ease the shortage of housing materials. The insistence of this pressure is indicated by the fact that the Forest Service is required, once a week, to report accomplishments in meeting planned timber sale objectives to its Washington office in order to keep the Secretary of Agriculture, Congress, and outside groups informed of progress in meeting timber cut commitments [Emphasis added].[38]

Developing counterpressures from conservationists seeking a more cautious timber management policy have temporarily weakened the timber industry's thrust. Indeed, the Forest Service acknowledged in a comprehensive 1972 report on nationwide timber supply and demand trends that "a new wave of concern over protection of the natural environment" will both limit the expansion of National Forest timber yield and require some modification of timber harvesting practices.[39] Whether or not the Forest Service translates these projections into management policy depends largely on the outcome of the National Forest debate in the political arena. And despite its new environmental pragmatism, the Forest Service remains, with its large discretion in National Forest matters, highly vulnerable to timber industry pressure. Without a clear Congressional mandate to govern Forest Service activities, the President can still issue directives calling for more cutting (see Chapter 4) and the President and Congress can continue to weight the Forest Service budget heavily in favor of timber production (see Chapter 5).

The scuttling in early 1972 of a proposed Executive Order limiting clearcutting on federal lands underscored the timber industry's ability to shape National Forest management policy—in this instance with the apparent acquiescence of the Forest Service. The proposed Order originated in the President's Council on Environmental Quality (CEQ). Following the Senate Subcommittee on Public Lands' inquiry into clearcutting in 1971, CEQ contracted with the deans of five forestry schools for studies of clearcutting in each major region of the country. The deans submitted their reports late last year. Like previous Forest Service management reviews, the reports endorsed clearcutting in theory, but acknowledged that its application had often abused the forest environment. According to a Congressional Research Service summary, "All the reports stressed the complexity of the problem, the need for changes in policy, and the need for continued research, but none recommended a complete ban on clearcutting. Four recommended zoning or classification." [40]

Dissatisfied with their quality,[41] CEQ sent photocopies of the reports to four forestry consultants and to the Forest Service and the Bureau of Land Management (BLM). On the basis of their comments and its own research, CEQ issued a position paper on November 22, 1971, declaring:

> Extensive studies of timber management on the public lands have indicated the need for a new, clear statement of policies to ensure protection of the ecological values of these lands . . . There is a substantial consensus on the need for certain uniform safeguards. These include strict limitations on the use of clearcutting as a means of harvesting timber.

The paper proposed that the President issue an Executive Order which would "establish a presumption against clearcutting except under specified conditions." [42] Such a pronouncement would be a clear departure from the recommendations of the Forest Service review teams and the Senate Subcommittee on Public Lands.[43]

CEQ asked the Forest Service and BLM to comment on the position paper. Both opposed the issuance of an Executive Order. According to counsel William T. Lake, CEQ's expert on clearcutting, this response was one of "Let us solve our own problems." The agencies also thought it wise to delay executive action until the President's Advisory

Panel on Timber and the Environment released its report.* CEQ revised the position paper and on December 14, 1971, again sent it to the Forest Service and BLM for review. The agencies repeated their previous objections, but, according to Lake, "They didn't convince us. We always agreed that they had the legal authority to restrict abuses. We thought it would give them a lot of boost to have a Presidential Order behind them."

Thus, before Christmas, Lake drafted an Executive Order for CEQ, entitled, "Environmental Guidelines for Timber Harvesting on the Public Lands." [45] It began by supporting governmental leadership in environmental forestry:

> The Government shall ensure that environmental considerations are weighed fully in all decisions made on the public lands, in order to produce a high sustained yield of goods and services without harm to the long-term environmental and resource value of those lands.

The guts of the Order, however, were contained in sections entitled, "Limitations on the Use of Clearcutting" and "Criteria for Timber Harvesting." The first section directed the Secretaries of Agriculture and Interior to develop and issue within one year regulations permitting clearcutting on public timberlands only under the following conditions:

(1) Clearcutting for the particular tree species and specific area in question must have a silvicultural justification.

---

* On September 2, 1971, President Nixon appointed a five-man panel to "advise the President on matters associated with increasing the Nation's supply of timber to meet growing housing needs while protecting and enhancing the quality of our environment." Its members are Frederick A. Seaton (Chairman), Secretary of the Interior in the second Eisenhower Administration; Stephen H. Spurr, forest-ecologist and president of the University of Texas at Austin; Marion Clawson, economist at Resources for the Future, Inc., Washington, D.C.; Ralph D. Hodges, Jr., executive vice-president of the National Forest Products Association; and Donald J. Zinn, zoology professor and past president of the National Wildlife Federation.

The panel was originally announced in a statement by the President, June 19, 1970. The President then waited fourteen months before appointing its members. The September 2, 1971, announcement of the appointments indicated that the panel would report to the President by July 1, 1972. Over a year later, as this book went to press, the panel report had just been submitted to the White House but not yet publicly released. [44] The repeated delays suggest that the Nixon Administration does not consider the solution of National Forest development conflicts particularly urgent.

(2) There will be no clearcutting in areas of outstanding scenic beauty, nor in areas where clearcutting would adversely affect existing or projected intensive recreational use or critical wildlife habitat.

(3) Clearcutting will not be used on sites where slope, elevation, and soil type, considered together, indicate severe erosion may result.

(4) No area will be clearcut unless there is assurance that the area can be regenerated promptly.

Under "Criteria for Timber Harvesting," the proposed Order directed the Forest Service and BLM to include in timber sale contracts detailed standards for road construction, timber cutting, slash disposal and site treatment, and regeneration. Timber purchasers would be required to post "a performance bond in an amount sufficient to ensure restoration of the area in the event the contract is not followed." The Order also directed the Forest Service and BLM to improve supervision of contracts, to solicit public participation in decision-making, to develop new technology for removing wood (including skyline, balloon, and helicopter methods), and to complete and adopt as soon as possible multiple-use management plans for all public forest lands.

Finally, the draft Order directed the Forest Service and BLM to identify within twenty-four months and protect "fragile areas that are unable to withstand timber harvesting or other intensive uses without significant environmental or resource damage." The concluding section of the draft Order indicated that the guidelines would not apply to timber sale contracts that had been concluded or for which bids had been accepted prior to the effective date of the guidelines. And that date would be one year after the signing of the Order.[46]

The proposed order had several advantages over the Forest Service's *Action Plan* and the guidelines of the Senate Subcommittee on Public Lands. First, it would have forced more care in the use of clearcutting by making it an unusual practice requiring extensive justification, rather than a routinely accepted harvesting tool. Second, the Order's limitations on clearcutting and its criteria for timber harvesting would have provided more specific policy

62 THE LAST STAND

guidance in forest management, while still leaving the details of implementation to the Forest Service and BLM. Finally, unlike the Forest Service plan or the Subcommittee guidelines, it would have had the force of law.

The Forest Service objected to each successive version of the proposed Order, which was revised a number of times up to January 12, 1972. Nevertheless, CEQ went ahead with plans to issue it through the President's annual message to Congress on the state of the environment in early February 1972. The Order was never issued. It fell victim to a remarkably blatant lobbying assault by the timber industry.

As is the custom with proposed Executive Orders, CEQ had circulated the draft clearcutting Order only among Forest Service, BLM, and other government officials. However, CEQ Chairman Russell Train told the Senate Appropriations Committee earlier this year, "During this review, a copy of the proposed order was apparently obtained by representatives of the forest industries." [47] CEQ was "extremely annoyed" at the leak, CEQ Counsel Lake said, especially when timber industry publications began warning that the proposed Order would stop the flow of timber from National Forest lands and severely damage the industry.[48] Letters from timber industry executives opposing the Order inundated the offices of CEQ, White House staffers, the Secretary of Agriculture, the Forest Service, and scores of Senators and Congressmen.

On Saturday, January 8, 1972, newly appointed Secretary of Agriculture Earl Butz telephoned James Turnbull, then executive vice-president of the National Forest Products Association. Butz asked Turnbull to summon industry leaders to Washington to discuss the proposed Order. He did *not* also telephone representatives of conservation, recreation, or professional forestry groups, or in any other way solicit their views.[49] In fact, they, unlike the industry leaders, did not see a copy of the Order until after it had been rejected.[50] At a Senate hearing, March 6, 1972, Senator Gale W. McGee questioned Secretary Butz about meeting exclusively with representatives of the timber industry:

> SENATOR MCGEE: Wouldn't you agree, Mr. Secretary, that this was a very lop-sided or one-sided type of consultation at a critical time?
> SECRETARY BUTZ: No sir, I would not agree to that. It

> may have been as far as I was concerned. But my
> primary concern really was with the Forest Service,
> with the forests, and with the harvest of timber.
> . . . We deal with many commodity groups, if I
> can call forestry a commodity. We deal with them
> all the time. We find it helpful. It is one of the ways
> that we get information.[51]

Secretary Butz met with the industry representatives in his office on January 10. Only *after* the meeting did the press, and thus the public, learn of either the proposed Executive Order, or the industry's already far-advanced campaign to prevent its issuance. On January 13, CEQ's William Lake announced that CEQ Chairman Train, Secretary Butz, and Secretary of the Interior Rogers C. B. Morton had decided to jettison the proposed Order.[52] In the intervening three days, what Senator McGee called "droves" of timber industry executives had descended on Washington to pressure Senators and Congressmen to oppose the Order. In an exchange at the Senate hearings in March, Senator McGee and Secretary Butz clashed over the Senator's use of the word "droves":

> SECRETARY BUTZ: I wouldn't say droves. We had a
> dozen of them here. You can define "drove" any way
> you want.
> SENATOR MCGEE: I was here at that time. I was be-
> sieged in the hallways. I mean droves.
> SECRETARY BUTZ: I thank you for entertaining them
> up here. It made my job easier. I just had a dozen.
> SENATOR MCGEE: It certainly made your job simpler,
> but I think it entitles us to raise some doubts about
> the way in which the decision to reverse that execu-
> tive order was arrived at.[53]

The content of the proposed clearcutting Executive Order had little to do with its scuttling. Fearful of even the slightest government regulation of timber harvesting, the timber industry stirred up effective Congressional opposition, not by arguing against the Order on its merits, but by threatening officeholders with election-year reprisals. Conservation groups, which occasionally wield consider-able clout,* this time were caught off-guard. While timber

---

* A majority in the House of Representatives, organized by leading conservationists, voted down the National Timber Supply Act in February 1970. Chapter 4 contains further details.

lobbyists, alerted by an unidentified federal official, were applying pressure to the President and Congress, the conservationists were still seeking a copy of the controversial Order. The leak of the draft Order to industry, and Secretary Butz's solicitation of advice from industry executives were crucial to the Order's downfall.

How industry obtained a copy of the Order is not clear. William T. Lake, the director of CEQ's effort, said that CEQ did not leak it to industry, and gave copies only to the White House, the Forest Service, and BLM. Why Secretary Butz sought the advice and lobbying assistance of industry representatives alone is more easily explained. Apparently, the Forest Service designed Butz's strategy. Lake said, "My impression is that the Forest Service was always closely involved. I consider the Forest Service and Secretary Butz one and the same in the discussions." [54] The fact that Butz had just assumed office, could not have known much about the issues, and must therefore have depended on the Forest Service to brief him lends credence to Lake's assertion.

Few of the participants in the controversy other than CEQ officials seemed to recognize the merits of the proposed Order. As *The New York Times* noted in an editorial, "The veiled threat and the general uproar over the proposed order served to obscure its import. . . . In recent years clearcutting has made alarming inroads where it ought never to have been allowed, and the Forest Service seems unable to arrest abuse of the practice which, with its approval, has spread so widely and dangerously." [55]

TECHNOLOGY AND THE FORESTS

Finally, the clearcutting controversy, like the National Forest debate in general, illustrates the current sway of technology over professional forestry, and the Forest Service in particular. The development of new forest cultivation and harvesting technologies, such as clearcutting, has reinforced the long-held view of some foresters that the forest is nothing more than a perpetual store of exploitable natural resources. Chief Pinchot espoused this narrow view: "Forestry is Tree Farming. . . . The purpose of Forestry, then, is to make the forest produce the largest possible amount of whatever crop or service will be most useful, and keep on producing it for generation after generation of men and trees." [56]

In the Forest Service's second and third decades, however, its foresters began taking the view, shared by many nonforesters today, that the forest is a fragile ecology vital as a whole to man apart from whatever material benefits it may confer on him. Guided by this view, the Forest Service set aside millions of acres of National Forest land as wilderness areas, acquired and reforested many denuded watersheds in the East, and attempted by example and later by seeking regulatory legislation to curb destructive clearcutting on private forest lands. [57]

After World War II, however, Pinchot's commodity view won reacceptance as new timber growing, harvesting, and processing technologies were developed to help meet the soaring demand for lumber. Forestry school curricula began emphasizing the science and economics of timber production. Consequently, the foresters entering the Forest Service tended less and less to take the holistic approach of their predecessors. By the 1960s, these men had become the leaders of the Forest Service. When they directed the application of new timber technology to boost National Forest timber yield, it is not surprising that nontimber National Forest values were shortchanged and occasionally forgotten altogether. Elizabeth Peelle of the Oak Ridge National Laboratory explains:

> Clearcutting was adopted in order to maximize growth and production, two agency goals. Much attention has been given to the mechanization of logging, planting, brush clearing, etc., and the requirements of bigger and more efficient machinery. It is probably no accident that the intolerance of new and bigger machinery for residual stands (the result of selection cutting) coincides with the adoption of clearcutting as the Forest Service's preferred policy in 1964. . . . Fragile ecosystems formerly inaccessible are now subject to massive disturbance by large machinery because of new technologies and roads. Steep slopes formerly considered unharvestable are cut because new techniques of terracing and artificial planting make reforestation a possibility. [58]

New technologies are often applied without sufficient prior consideration of their potentially disastrous impacts.

Clearcutting was no exception. It took a series of highly vocal public protests and deep rumblings in Congress to impel the Forest Service to acknowledge—let alone measure or attempt to mitigate—the visual and environmental impacts of its widespread clearcutting. The agency has since recognized the *visual* damage wreaked by clearcutting and has taken steps to control it in the future, although the Service did make the preposterous remark that "clearcuttings can be used to provide variety to the landscape and enhance the visual resource." [59] Thus far the Forest Service has refused to limit clearcutting in deference to the scarcity of data on its long-term impacts on the natural environment.

Scientists and conservationists have charged that clearcutting may in the long run destroy aquatic life, trigger massive erosion, deplete soil nutrients, reduce watershed capacity, and disrupt the micro-climate.[60] The Forest Service responds that "currently available information" indicates that the long-term impacts of clearcutting, if properly practiced, will be minimal.[61] But data on the subject is regarded even by a prominent Forest Service consultant as seriously inadequate.[62] Until current knowledge is greatly augmented, the Forest Service is courting disaster with the present level of clearcutting.

The Forest Service has also been slow to consider the effect of clearcutting on nontimber uses of the National Forests. Few people enjoy hiking, camping, or picnicking in an area scalped by clearcutting. If the area happens to be on the side of a mountain, the highly visible scar may greatly diminish the recreational value of surrounding forest lands as well. Since clearcutting wipes out the existing forest and tears up the landscape, clearcut areas take years to regain the look of a healthy forest. If, as frequently happens, initial attempts at reforestation fail, visual impairment may persist even longer.

Clearcutting also conflicts with watershed maintenance and wildlife habitat protection. "Clearcutting tends to produce relatively uniform forests lacking the diversity needed for a good mix of wildlife," asserts Professor Leon Minkler of the State University of New York's College of Forestry.[63] Clearcutting also disrupts the flow from National Forest watersheds. Though it may boost water yield for several years, a permanent diminution frequently follows.[64] Siltation of forest streams due to clearcutting can kill aquatic life, clog irrigation systems, and pollute municipal water supplies.[65]

Critics have even questioned whether the two factors which led the Forest Service to apply clearcutting in the first place—economic and biological efficiency—still justify its use in all regions and on all tree species. The Forest Service would doubtless undertake far less clearcutting if it took into account the full cost of reforestation and measures to mitigate the damage done to the environment and nontimber forest uses; clearcutting would be too expensive.[66]

Some foresters have challenged the Forest Service's contention that the regeneration of "shade-intolerant" tree species—including many of the valuable softwoods—requires clearcutting to open the new forest to sunlight. The critics have presented evidence that shelterwood and group selection cutting would permit equally effective forest reproduction without the extreme visual and environmental degradation that accompanies clearcutting.[67] Even if, as most foresters contend, clearcutting is an appropriate, environmentally acceptable practice with certain tree species and growing sites, it must be recognized as a massive, violent assault on forest ecosystems requiring the most careful planning and the most sensitive application.

The clearcutting controversy illustrates the glaring need to learn more about the long-term impacts of various timber management practices. More generous funding from Congress and the President is essential. In the meantime, the record of short-run environmental catastrophes following clearcutting suggests the wisdom of greatly curtailing its use in the National Forests until information on long-term effects becomes available. A clear lesson of the controversy is that no new technology should be applied before completion of a thorough inquiry into its potential impacts —environmental as well as economic.

The clearcutting controversy further demonstrates that the public is greatly dissatisfied with present National Forest management and will demand a major role in future management decision-making. Of course, the controversy shows with equal vividness that the public's, and more recently the Forest Service's own, attempts to secure policy improvements can still founder on the rocks of the influential timber lobby.

The inadequacy of the purely resource-oriented forester also emerges from the clearcutting controversy. A new forester is needed whose first concern is the preservation of the forest as a complex, fragile ecology vital to man in its entirety as well as in its resource parts. To avoid future controversies, the new Forest Service professional must encourage, and be guided largely, by the involvement of the public—including individuals and citizens' groups as well as Congress and the President—in substantive National Forest decision-making.

4
♣ ♣

The Forest Service Mandate:
Cut at Will

*Harvesting timber is like harvesting wheat—
but growing timber is measured in decades instead of months. When timber is cut there is
a temporary loss of beauty. There is also the
promise of what is to come, a thinned new
forest replacing the old. The pattern of management you see here assures that future generations of Americans will always have timber
—and natural beauty.[1]*

> *Forest Service sign at one entrance
> to the Monongahela National Forest
> in West Virginia*

Rampant clearcutting is only the most glaring of the timber lobbyists' accomplishments. Thanks to them, increases
in the amount of timber harvesting also threaten the ability of the National Forests to maintain current yields of
water, recreational opportunities, wildlife habitat, and
range—as well as timber. According to a Forest Service
study released in March 1973, ceilings on timber cutting
in some National Forests may be as much as 30 percent too
high.[2] And there are documented instances of actual cutting, over entire Forests and Forest Service Regions,
exceeding even these inflated limits.[3]

Timber industry lobbying has paid off largely because
Forest Service foresters are peculiarly vulnerable to political pressure. Every forester, whether employed by the
gigantic Weyerhaeuser Company, the Forest Service, or
Farmer Small, must inject policy constraints as well as
biological survey information into his determination of
desired annual harvesting levels. But the industry forester
has a far easier time than his counterpart at the Forest
Service. The industry forester need worry only about maximizing dollar return on dollar investment. His policy con-

69

straints—tangible economic concepts readily applicable to the tangible biological data collected—are fully defined for him by the free market and his company's financial planners. The hapless Forest Service forester, on the other hand, must design a timber production program that guarantees a "sustained yield" of timber and the other renewable resources of the National Forests, provide for "multiple use"—not simply efficient timber use—of the forests "in the combination that will best meet the needs of the American people," and "preserve the forests from destruction." [4] Left to interpret these constraints and tailor timber production activities to meet them—all decisions which, in the absence of clear statutory standards, are highly subjective—the Forest Service forester makes easy prey for the timber lobbyist and his political friends.

I.   The "Sustained Yield" Constraint on Logging

Guiding statutes, departmental regulations, and agency directives may be vague, but the Forest Service forester does not make timber management decisions in a policy vacuum. One major policy constraint is the requirement in the Multiple Use–Sustained Yield Act of 1960 that the National Forests be managed for a "sustained yield" of their timber and other renewable resources. Sustained yield is defined in the statute as "the achievement and maintenance in perpetuity of a high-level annual or regular periodic output of the various renewable resources of the National Forests without impairment of the productivity of the land." [5] An earlier statute, the Organic Administration Act of 1897, identifies as a principal purpose of the National Forests "to furnish a continuous supply of timber for the use and necessities of citizens of the United States." [6]

In plain language, these statutes authorize the Forest Service to remove timber from the National Forests at annual rates preserving the forests' capacity to produce timber indefinitely for the needs of the American people. The Secretary of Agriculture's regulations (published in the *Code of Federal Regulations*) and the Chief of the Forest Service's directives (published in the *Forest Service Manual*) expand on the statutory requirement of sustained yield.

The Secretary of Agriculture's regulations authorize the

Forest Service to "develop an orderly program of timber sales designed to obtain the regular harvest of national forest timber at allowable cutting rates as determined by timber management plans. . . ." These plans, one for each National Forest, must "be based on the principle of sustained yield," and "provide, so far as feasible, an even flow of national forest timber in order to facilitate the stabilization of communities and of opportunities for employment." "Even flow" means the maintenance of the same or higher output of timber from one year or management period to the next, forever. The Secretary's regulations further require that the plans "provide for coordination of timber production and harvesting with other uses of National Forest land in accordance with the principles of multiple-use management." Finally, to implement the even-flow policy and to prevent excessive cutting in any one period, the timber management plans must "establish the allowable cutting rate which is the maximum amount of timber which may be cut from the National Forest lands within the [management] unit by years or other periods." [7]

These regulations, designed to elucidate the hazy statutory concepts of "continuous supply" and "sustained yield," raise more questions than they answer. The even-flow requirement, for instance, gives sustained yield a definitive interpretation, but under what circumstances will that interpretation be deemed "feasible"? The coordination-of-uses requirement appears to go far in preventing conflicts between logging and other National Forest uses, but through the application of what system of weights or other set of standards will this trying task be accomplished? The allowable-cutting-rate requirement seems a prudent safeguard against Bunyanesque overcutting, but is the rate to be a ceiling on the volume actually harvested in a particular year or other period, or merely a ceiling on the volume sold during that time, regardless of the speed with which it is harvested and removed? And how is this most important guarantor of sustained yield to be calculated? The regulation-writers, like the statute-makers, provide few answers; instead they pass the buck, this time to the Forest Service.

Despite its apparent thoroughness (the timber management planning chapter numbers forty pages and the entire set of loose-leaf binders covers ten feet of shelf space), the

Forest Service Manual leaves the most basic aspects of timber planning to the discretion of field officers.[8] For identifying the timber-production land base—the controlling step in the preparation of a timber management plan—the *Manual* provides the forest supervisor with only the vaguest of classification criteria. Drawing upon information in "multiple use plans, resource inventories, and other records," the supervisor isolates first the "land," then the "forest land," then the "productive forest land," and finally the "commercial forest land." The *Manual* assists the supervisor with a "classification key" for productive forest land (see Appendix 4-1).

Commercial forest land, the only National Forest land involved in timber production, is designated as "regulated" or "unregulated." Regulated commercial forest land—that which "can contribute to systematic timber production under sustained yield principles"—is subdivided into "standard," "special," and "marginal." The standard component of the regulated commercial forest land—identified by both environmental and economic standards—is the

> area on which crops of industrial wood can be grown and harvested with adequate protection of the forest resources under the usual provisions of the timber sale contract. . . . This area is capable of producing timber crops that have a reasonable probability of demand under the accessibility and economic conditions projected for a 10-year plan period, even though portions of the area may not be developed during this period.

The special component of the regulated commercial forest land is the

> area that is recognized in the multiple use plan as needing specially designed treatment of the timber resource to achieve landscape or other key resource objectives. Areas where timber management activities are informally delayed pending multiple use planning studies and management decisions, travel and water influence zones, peripheral portions of developed sites, and classified recreation areas, such as Whiskeytown-Shasta Trinity National Recreation Area where timber harvest is a secondary or minor management objective should be included in this classification.

The marginal component of the regulated commercial forest land is the

> area not qualifying as standard or special components primarily because of excessive development cost, low product values, or resource protection constraints. Included may be drainages requiring unusual logging techniques, such as helicopters, areas where harvesting is blocked until government constructed roads are in place, or species types not presently in demand. Also included is the backlog of nonstocked areas that would otherwise be classed as standard, but are in need of reforestation that cannot be accomplished with Knutson-Vandenberg Act funds.

"Unregulated" commercial forest land—that which "will not be organized for timber production under sustained yield principles"—includes experimental forests, recreation and administrative sites "where timber harvest is permissible but not a goal of management" (these sites are to be distinguished from the much larger "travel and water influence" recreation zones, which are classified as special regulated commercial forest land), and "isolated tracts of commercial forest land so completely remote from manufacturing centers that organizing and scheduling sustained periodic harvest is impractical." [9]

This complex stratification of forest land assumes major importance when the planner begins calculating the National Forest's "potential yield" and "programed allowable harvest." Before these concepts are discussed, it should therefore be recognized that the *Manual*'s definitions cited above are so imprecise—perhaps unavoidably—that the planner's classification decisions will be highly subjective. Some of his decisions, of course, are actually made by others: the land and the water in a National Forest, for instance, are clearly distinguished, and productive forest land included in a designated Wilderness Area is necessarily considered "reserved." In addition, the forest's multiple-use plan theoretically determines, among other things, how much of the forest's regulated commercial forest land will be placed in the "special" category. But, as will be discussed in Chapter 5, the formulation of the multiple-use plan itself involves many subjective judgments about the extent and intensity of logging desirable, and the harvesting and utilization technology and markets for wood available, in the forest. Moreover, with new timber-management plans being formulated before new multiple-use plans in some forests, it is unclear how the multiple-use plans will be able to determine the "special-regulated" component recognized in the timber-management plans—as the *Manual* requires. Where the timber-management planner, unassisted by prior statutory, regulatory, or multiple-use planning decisions, must make an important classification decision—for instance, which commercial forest land is so fragile environmentally that it should be placed in the "marginal" category for more cautious handling, and which land is so remote from manufacturing centers that it should be designated "unregulated"—the *Manual* offers only vague standards. The danger is great that these decisions will be arbitrary or, especially in the subdividing of commercial forest land, where the planner must make economic as well as environmental assessments, biased in favor of expanding the land under intensive timber management.

Before the land in a National Forest can be classified, or the forest's timber yield calculated, an "inventory" must be taken. The *Manual* details the information to be obtained —the volume and condition of standing timber and its growth rates, and the identification of different "forest types" and biotic/climatic/soil-condition "sites"—and how and when (preferably in conjunction with the decennial nationwide forest survey, but in any case at least once every ten years) to obtain it.[10]

The inventory techniques prescribed by the *Manual* and related Forest Service handbooks, however, are extremely imprecise. The entire forest is photographed from the air, sample data from scattered small areas are obtained through ground surveys, and this data is extrapolated for all the other areas that appear from the photographs to be similar to the sample areas. Recalling their own experiences in the agency and in private industry, some academic foresters and conservationists suspect that Forest Service inventories contain serious flaws.[11] Forest Service estimates of growth rates for different tree species under varying site conditions and management practices—determined on the basis of information from sample growth plots which may, or may not, be typical of the entire forest—are thought to be especially vulnerable to error. Since the ultimate aim of sustained-yield timber management is to balance annual cut with annual growth, growth rate estimates are key factors in the establishment of harvesting levels. The skeptical academic foresters contend that the Forest Service could eliminate many of the inventories' flaws by switching to the more exact survey techniques available in forestry research literature and used by some industry timberland owners. But without the underpinning of an inventory completely independent of the Forest Service—and none has ever been conducted, mostly because of the estimated quarter-million-dollar cost—the foresters have been unwilling to challenge the Forest Service's inventory figures authoritatively.

Following the timber inventory, the forest supervisor must decide what rotations—ages at which trees or stands of trees are harvested—will be used to determine cutting rates. The *Manual* used to define rotation only as the "culmination of mean annual increment," the age at which a tree's annual growth begins to taper off. This objective, biological definition was supplemented in 1965 by a subjective one, tied to economic demand, if to anything: "rotations should be the minimum periods which will ensure reaching the timber size and quality objectives and the other forest uses objectives." [12] The new definition jeopardizes the sustained yield capacity of the old-growth National Forests of the West. For instance, if planners decided that the timber size and quality objectives in a particular region—say, the production of pulpwood for paper manufacture—demanded that a forest containing mammoth, 200-year-old trees be managed on an 50-year rotation, neither the quantity nor the quality of the forest's timber yield would be sustainable on an even flow basis. The quantity would drop off drastically after 50 years because the old-growth would have been completely removed and the 1/50 of the second-growth forest then ready to harvest would not have accumulated nearly the volume of the final 1/50 of the old growth harvested the preceding year. The quality would diminish because 50-year-old trees lack the clear grain and strong fiber of two-hundred-year-old trees. A rotation closer to the two-hundred-year age of the trees now standing—perhaps one based on the "culmination of mean annual increment"—would preserve more quantity and quality in the forest's timber flow.

Using the land classifications, inventory data, selected rotation ages, his knowledge of growth-inducing "intensive forestry" measures, logging technology, and economic demand, and other information, the planner calculates the "potential yield" of the National Forest. The potential yield, calculated for the ten years of the timber management plan, is:

> the maximum harvest that could be planned to achieve the optimum perpetual sustained yield harvesting level attainable with intensive forestry on regulated areas considering the productivity of the land, conventional logging technology, standard cultural treatments, and inter-relationship with other resource uses and the environment.[13]

The Forest Service has developed a computer program, "Timber RAM," to assist the planner with the actual computations. It should be noted that potential yield, like the "allowable cut" of the pre-May 1972 *Manual*, is calculated only for the regulated commercial forest land area. Unlike its predecessor, however, the potential yield of a National Forest is the sum of the separately-calculated potential yields of the standard, special, and marginal components of the regulated commercial forest area. The increased precision in the current calculations should make them more accurate than the old ones and discourage borrowing on the growth of one tract of timber to rationalize the overcutting of another—unrelated by location, forest type, or site to the first.

The potential yield limits the volume harvested cumulatively over the 10-year plan period, but, unlike the old allowable cut, does not limit the volume harvested in any one year. Indeed, it constitutes as much a cutting goal as a cutting limit, since it is premised upon the application of intensive forestry practices that may, in fact, never be applied. Potential yield is modified during the plan period only in response to changes in the regulated commercial forest land base (caused, for instance, by new wilderness withdrawals), or the structure of the forest (caused, for instance, by a fire or insect attack), or the invention of new forestry or logging technology. Potential yield is not adjusted in response to the application or nonapplication of projected intensive forestry practices.

The new ceiling on annual harvesting—which appears to satisfy the Secretary of Agriculture's maximum-cut regulation—is the "programed allowable harvest." It is defined in the *Manual* as:

> that part of the potential yield that is scheduled for a specific year. It is based on current demand, funding, silvicultural practices, and multiple use considerations. . . . Where components of the programed allowable harvest are less than the potential yield, it will be a continuing objective to remove the barriers and work the programed allowable harvest up to the full potential yield.[14]

The programed allowable harvest is, in effect, (1) one-tenth of the potential yield plus unharvested volumes accrued from previous years in the plan period, minus (2) any increases in harvesting based on growth-inducing intensive forestry measures which were scheduled but have not been accomplished to date, minus (3) that part of the resultant volume whose sale preparation and administration cannot be financed within the current year's budget. If the cost of preparing and administering timber sales proves more costly than expected, the full programed allowable harvest may not actually be harvested.

It is important to note that the programed allowable harvest cannot be increased in proportion to the projected effects of intensive forestry measures which have merely been planned or even funded, but not yet accomplished. The programed allowable harvest cannot be raised, for instance, in response to the reforestation of nonstocked lands until new trees are planted and clearly take hold. A supplement to the *Manual* issued on May 1, 1973, emphasizes the Forest Service's conservative approach to this so-called "allowable cut effect":

> Increments to potential sustained yield for the various components together with the silvicultural or technological practice required to achieve such increments should be identified and specified as to acres and type of treatment, size or species to be utilized or logging method required. Such increments in yield should be programed only insofar as the practices required are employed in ongoing programs. This will ensure that credit is not taken for given practices until the work is accomplished.[15]

It might still be argued that before taking credit for intensive forestry measures, the Forest Service should wait the one to ten years it takes to discern whether or not the measures have stimulated timber growth to the extent anticipated.

Several provisions of the timber management planning chapter of the *Manual* could be interpreted—given the right combination of economic conditions, political pressures, and personal biases—as permitting faster-than-sustainable cutting. Due to the vagueness of the *Manual*'s land-use classification criteria, for instance, the planner could designate as standard regulated commercial forest land—the land intensively managed for timber production —land which, in fact, could not be regenerated after harvesting of its old-growth timber. Add the distortions caused by faulty inventory data, overly optimistic growth rate estimates, and rotations artificially shortened by timber "size and quality objectives," and the forest's mature timber could be exhausted within several decades.

The threat seems the more real because of the instances of serious overcutting in the past which the Forest Service and others have recently brought to light. In the late 1960s, for example, the Forest Service quietly auctioned off to a single logging company 3.75 billion board feet of standing timber—one-third of the annual allowable harvest nationwide—in Alaska's virgin Tongass National Forest. The contract included transfer of National Forest land to the company for the building of a processing plant and called for harvesting of the purchased timber, mostly by clearcutting, over the next 50 years. Suspicious of the very magnitude of the timber sale, the Sierra Club sent its staff forester, Gordon Robinson, to Alaska to check the Forest Service's inventory data. He concluded that the Forest Service's estimates of timber volume were much too high, and that its confidence in the forest's ability to regenerate itself rapidly was scarcely justified. As a result, the Sierra Club sued the Forest Service for violating the Multiple Use-Sustained Yield Act. The Forest Service denied the charges of overcutting and convinced the U.S. District Court to decide the case in its favor. The Sierra Club appealed, but before the U.S. Court of Appeals could hand down an opinion, the contracting company announced that a study conducted by its own consultants had turned up errors in the Forest Service's inventory data which could indeed result in overcutting. At the Sierra Club's request, the Court of Appeals, in March 1973, sent the case back to the District Court for a new trial. The Sierra Club has postponed further legal action while the Forest Service and the logging company renegotiate the timber sale contract.[16]

The Forest Service may be overcutting National Forests throughout the country as a result of its inclusion in timber management plans of lands which, because of their environmental fragility or poor regenerative ability, cannot support sustained-yield timber production. A 1971 Forest Service survey of six western National Forests indicated that the "area suitable and available for growing tree crops" in the forests was "22 percent less than had been previously estimated." This huge error led to the computing of allowable harvests far above the sustained-yield capacity of the forests involved.[17] A more comprehensive study, reported in draft form by the Forest Service in March 1973, suggests that greatly inflated allowable harvests are the rule, not the exception, throughout the National Forest System. Reclassification under current land use criteria of the lands constituting twelve National Forests in Montana, Washington, Oregon, and California, the *Forest Regulation Study* concluded, would necessitate a 30-percent reduction in the forests' allowable harvests.[18]

Finally, even where the allowable harvests have gone unchallenged, Forest Service field officials have occasionally permitted the volume sold for harvesting to surpass the ceiling. In the Pacific Northwest Region (Washington and Oregon), which contributes one-third of the National Forest System's annual timber output, the volume sold exceeded the Region's allowable harvest in nine of the last ten years.[19] A special Forest Service task force, reviewing management of Montana's Bitterroot National Forest, discovered in 1970 that the allowable harvest had been exceeded substantially from 1966 through 1969, with especially heavy cutting of ponderosa pine causing a decline in that valuable species's future annual yields. The task force attributed this irresponsible management to "most insistent pressure" from the Washington office of the Forest Service "to increase the timber cut on the National Forests in order to make more timber available to ease the shortage of housing materials." [20]

II.   The "Multiple Use" Constraint on Logging

Statutes and regulations place a second major constraint on National Forest timber production: it must be coordinated with other uses of the National Forests. The Multiple Use–Sustained Yield Act of 1960 directs the Secretary of Agriculture "to develop and administer the renewable surface resources of the national forests for multiple use. . . . Due consideration shall be given to the relative values of the various resources in particular areas." The statute designates, as purposes for which the forests are to be administered, "outdoor recreation, timber, range, watershed, and wildlife and fish purposes." [21] But the statute does not explain what weights are to be assigned to the "relative values" nor what action shall be deemed "due consideration." The degree to which nontimber use considerations are to limit the amount of timber harvesting in the National Forests is left to the subjective determination of the Forest Service. No agency exercising such extensive authority under such loose guidelines can avoid being besieged by pressure groups. And none therefore can avoid, however much it might want to, heeding and, over time, acceding to the demands of the most powerful group. In the case of the Forest Service, that group is the timber industry. Due to the industry's influence in the White House and Congress, the Forest Service has been enticed to establish cutting rates much higher than many Americans, if they were consulted, would find desirable.*

Four events illustrate the Forest Service's reluctance to recognize the multiple-use constraint on the amount of logging in the National Forests: the agency's uncritical adoption of the "intensive forestry" techniques used in tree farming; the timber industry-White House-Forest Service attempt to launch behind Congress's back an accelerated harvesting program for the National Forests; the Forest Service's utter disregard for nontimber uses in planning the 50-percent increase in annual cutting; and the agency's

* Chapter 5 contains a more extensive discussion of multiple-use management.

sluggish response to calls for more wilderness preservation in the National Forests.

AN INDUSTRY PROPOSAL:
"INTENSIVE MANAGEMENT"

On private lands, the timber industry has always harvested timber at rates exceeding what would be their allowable cut, with little thought of replacing the trees it felled. Today, at least on its own old-growth lands, the industry is still cutting timber at a feverish pace, but as a calculated step in the long-term, sustained-yield management of their lands. By wiping out most of its old-growth timber, the industry can plant new forests of genetically improved tree species which, in the long run, will yield harvestable timber much faster.

Looking for additional timber to supply its mills in the meantime, the industry has proposed that the Forest Service likewise place old-growth National Forest lands under "intensive management." As rapidly as its chain saws can cut and its sawmills process, the industry wants the Forest Service to convert the fifty million acres of "decaying" old-growth timber under its management into "thrifty" young forests capable of greatly outproducing their forbears.

The industry's logic founders on the policy considerations basic to National Forest timber management. First, the public interest in a steady supply of wood products and in the economic stability of logging communities—as well as the intent, if not the letter, of guiding statutes—requires that the timber output of the National Forests each year equal or exceed the previous year's output, forever. Intensive management, however, generally involves a sharp decline in timber harvests during the several decades following removal of the old growth and before the maturing of the new—a decidedly *uneven* flow. The *Forest Regulation Study*, released in 1973, shows that annual yields can be significantly increased within several decades without the usual drop-off only if harvesting is accelerated gradually and in proportioned response to the implementation of various growth improvement measures, and not immediately and sharply, as the industry would like.[22]

Second, placing old-growth forests under intensive management greatly reduces their huge inventories of standing timber. The fast-growing replacement forests are managed on short rotation: profit considerations dictate their harvest long before they have accumulated the massive amounts of wood fiber found in the natural old-growth stands. As a result, annual yield is greater than before conversion to intensive management, but the forests no longer contain old-growth reserves. It would be unfair to private timberland owners and contrary to the public policy of fostering private timber production to ask the timber industry to keep such reserves. But it would be shortsighted and possibly catastrophic for the Forest Service to liquidate the old-growth reserves in the National Forests and thus weaken the government's ability to cope with timber supply emergencies.[23]

Third, intensive management of the National Forests, at least at the level proposed by the industry, would require intolerable increases in the acreage and frequency of timber harvests. Broad application of any of the intensive harvesting methods—clearcutting, shelterwood cutting, or seed-tree cutting—would sacrifice many of the valuable non-timber benefits derived by millions of Americans from the National Forests. Additional thinning operations would further disrupt nontimber uses. The extensively documented environmental damage resulting from careless use of herbicides and pesticides suggests that the large-scale use of chemical fertilizer in the National Forests also might backfire ecologically. Perhaps worst of all, intensive forestry would reduce to tree farms the wild and scenic woodlands which today harbor rare vegetation and wildlife and supply much of the country's rising demand for clean water and recreational open space.

Fourth, intensive management entails the risk that once all the old growth has been harvested, the intensive forestry measures designed to accelerate tree growth may fail. The risk is especially grave on the National Forests. Many of their old-growth stands occupy sites whose relatively poor climate, terrain, and soil composition would severely inhibit the accelerated regrowth which allegedly justifies cutting them in the first place.

Brushing aside these major policy considerations, the Forest Service, in 1970 (before it launched the *Forest Regulation Study* mentioned above), hastily put together a plan to expand the annual sawtimber output of the National

Forests by fifty percent within a decade, justifying the rapid increase in harvesting with the application of intensive forestry practices.[24] An expanded "unregulated cut" and new thinning and salvage efforts would provide part of the proposed 7.4-billion-board-foot increase. The rest—3.4 billion board feet annually—would be achieved by speeding the liquidation of 52.6 million acres of old-growth timber. Under this plan, *the Forest Service would level (mostly by clearcutting) almost a third of the National Forests in the next sixty-nine years.* At present cutting rates, the process will take ninety-three years.[25]

The plan, inaptly entitled the "Environmental Program for the Future," prescribed major thinning, reforestation, tree fertilization, and other stand improvement measures. These, the Forest Service contended, would boost the growth rate of young timber sufficiently over the sixty-nine-year conversion period to permit continued harvesting at the accelerated levels in the seventieth and succeeding years. If the activities to boost growth proved successful, the plan would maintain an even flow of timber one-and-a-half times the present flow.

As will shortly be discussed, the Forest Service released the Environmental Program at the behest of the White House and the timber industry, and in the wake of Congress's clear refusal to authorize a similar plan by statute. Moreover, the Forest Service gave what many of its own officials conceded was inadequate consideration to the plan's impact on nontimber forest values. Considering that the plan involves the accelerated cutting of a primeval forested area larger than Maine, Vermont, New Hampshire, Massachusetts, Rhode Island, Connecticut, New Jersey, Delaware, and Maryland combined, its impact will not be small.

In the absence of the necessary funding and in response to criticism, the Forest Service has been revising the plan. The second edition of the Environmental Program will be more detailed, will present a range of new management options, and will "consider to a larger extent impacts on the environment." The Forest Service official in charge of "Phase II," Director of Program and Policy Analysis Adrian M. Gilbert, "won't exclude, nor will I include" the possibility that the revised program will also call for a speedup in the harvesting of the old-growth National Forest lands,[26]

but ongoing management activities and another agency proposal suggest that it will. In the February 1973 issue of
the *Journal of Forestry*, the Forest Service's Director of
Timber Management noted, "In planning the possible
future allowable harvest on a national forest, we are beginning to project full application of all of the intensive
management measures we know how to practice." [27] With
each succeeding increment in funding and personnel, a
computerized information, mapping, and management analysis system will suggest to the Forest Service manager new
intensive practices to stimulate timber growth and permit
an increase in allowable cut. Eventually, the system will
make annual adjustments in the allowable cut of every National Forest, in line with changes in the timberland base,
modified nontimber use needs, and technological advances
in tree harvesting and wood utilization.

In its 1972 report, *The Outlook for Timber in the United
States*, the Forest Service detailed an intensive management plan remarkably similar to the Environmental Program.[28] The report identifies several million acres of bare
or sparsely wooded National Forest land on which intensive
management would return five percent or more on added
costs. The increased annual harvests which this intensification would permit would come in the form of accelerated
liquidation of the western old-growth National Forest
stands. The *Outlook* report, however, neglects to provide
timber volume, acreage, location, or timing figures. Re-
portedly, this aspect of the proposal—in the long run, its
most important aspect—will be developed in later studies.[29]

These recent developments convey the alarming impression that a decision which will greatly affect the present
generation and many to come—whether or not to level the
old-growth stands in the National Forests and, if so, how
rapidly—has been delegated to a computer and a small
team of forest economists. After a year of informed deliber-
ation, Congress decisively rejected an accelerated timber
cutting plan only three years ago (see below). Surely, if
the idea is to be revived, it should be Congress, not a computer, that decides whether public recreational opportunities are to be curtailed permanently in order to achieve a
small increase, of questionable necessity, in the nation's
timber output.

POLITICKING FOR EXPANDED TIMBER PRODUCTION

In the late 1960s, sharp rises in lumber and plywood prices —discussed in Chapter 2—touched off a fierce Congressional debate over the level of National Forest timber production. The timber industry, with the support of the homebuilding industry, decided to take advantage of the inflation crisis to press for major, long-term increases in National Forest timber cutting. As noted in Chapter 2, the lobbyists' arguments lacked substance. Nevertheless, their draft legislation won the sponsorship of numerous Senators and Congressmen. The National Timber Supply Act would have established a "high timber yield fund." [30] Into the fund would flow the now approximately $325 million per year in National Forest timber sales receipts. Appropriations from the fund would finance intensive management practices— reforestation, thinning, and fertilization—aimed at spurring National Forest timber growth. The Act also would have directed the Forest Service to boost allowable cut on the basis of these anticipated growth increases.

The Forest Service played no part in drafting the original industry bill, introduced in the House and Senate in early 1969.[31] At the House hearings on the bill in May 1969, however, the agency recommended a remarkably similar substitute. Unlike the industry bill, it contained a provision promising continued adherence to the revered Multiple Use–Sustained Yield Act of 1960. But it kept the "high timber yield fund." [32] Assisted by such a fund, then Chief Cliff told a Senate hearing in October 1969, "We could increase timber harvests on the National Forests over 7 billion board feet in the next decade." [33] That would have boosted allowable cut by fifty percent.

After presenting the substitute bill to Congress, however, the Forest Service seemed to have second thoughts about its potentially negative impact on multiple-use management. While refusing to work against the bill—White House pressure and its own belief in intensive management and eagerness for a guaranteed source of operating funds were strong deterrents—the Forest Service did refrain from lobbying for it.*

* In 1972 and again in 1973, the Forest Service went still further and testified against bills, supported by timber lobbyists, to create a revolving fund for intensified National Forest timber production.[34]

If the Forest Service would not stop the bill, several national conservation groups were determined to do so. Led by Brock Evans, Washington, D.C., representative of the Sierra Club, they quickly mobilized national opinion against the bill in late 1969 and organized a Congressional counterattack. According to the Forest Service, the opposition of former U.S. Representative Wayne Aspinall (Democrat of Colorado), the influential chairman of the House Interior Committee, "was also a key factor in the bill being blocked." Aspinall, however, shared none of the conservationists' misgivings about the contents of the bill. He wanted only to delay Congressional consideration of intensified federal land management until his committee—a rival, in forestry matters, of the Agriculture Committee, which had handled the timber supply bill—could come up with more comprehensive legislation.[35] In any case, on February 26, 1970, the House of Representatives killed the National Timber Supply Act by voting 228–150 not to consider it.[36]

The defeat of the timber supply bill did not extinguish the industry's campaign to increase the cut on the National Forests. The lobbyists instead sought help from the White House. Ignoring Congress's rejection of an accelerated timber cutting program, the Nixon Administration decided to implement essentially the same program by administrative fiat. This time the Forest Service actively assisted.

In March 1969, as the legislative debate was beginning, the Forest Service set up the Forests and Related Resources (FARR) study group. Its task was to draw up a ten-year National Forest development plan. For months it focused exclusively on the problem of increasing timber production. On May 21, 1969, the Forest Service's Timber Management Division supplied a draft plan proposing a fifty-percent—7-billion-board-foot—increase in National Forest timber output within ten years.[37] (No one suggested this figure to the Forest Service. Drawing on the data in a 1968 study, the Forest Service had been considering a seven-billion-board-foot increase since March 1969.[38]) Meanwhile, the President's interagency Task Force on Softwood Lumber and Plywood had convened to discuss how to hold down spiraling lumber prices. Like FARR, the task force centered its attention on increasing the timber yield of the National Forests. On April 3, 1969, its staff working group, which included a top Forest Service official, requested an action plan from the Forest Service.[39]

The Forest Service submitted its report, "Possibilities for Meeting Future Demands for Softwood Timber in the United States," on August 1, 1969. The report indicated that under intensive management, the National Forests could yield 7.4 billion board feet more timber per year by 1980 than they were producing in 1968,[40] essentially the same figure mentioned in the FARR document and in former Chief Cliff's May 1969 testimony to Congress.* The working group endorsed the Forest Service report and forwarded it to the members of the Presidential task force, which also endorsed it in an October 1969 report to the Cabinet Committee on Economic Policy: "Increases of 7 to 8 billion board feet in annual timber harvest can be achieved over the next decade. . . ."[42]

The White House, in league with the timber industry, provided the initial impetus for administrative action to bypass Congress. On April 17, 1970, two months after the House of Representatives discarded the National Timber Supply Act, then special counsel to the President Charles W. Colson pushed the "administrative approach" in a memorandum to the chairman of the Presidential task force:

> In accordance with our conversation this afternoon, I am enclosing a white paper which has been prepared by the timber people, so it should be read with their obvious bias in mind. It does suggest, however, an administrative approach which has considerable merit. . . . Personally, I am convinced that we are better off this way than walking back into the hurricane that will ensue in the Congress.[43]

The industry "white paper" urged the application of intensive management practices to increase timber yield from the National Forests. The Forest Service itself had suggested identical action in its 1969 "Possibilities" paper.

---

* Although the Forest Service has not acknowledged it publicly, the FARR accelerated cutting program also includes more than *tripling* the annual yield of *convertible products* (timber of lesser size and quality than sawtimber, usually used for pulpwood) from the current 1.669 billion board feet to 5.131 billion board feet. As a result, *the plan would increase overall allowable cut by 67 percent*—considerably more than the publicized 50-percent increase in annual sawtimber yield.[41]

Nevertheless, the white paper chastised the agency for showing too little enthusiasm for timber production:

> Individual National Forest Supervisors, Regional Foresters, and the Chief need to be persuaded of the importance of timber production. This function of the National Forests has slipped badly in priority in the past ten years due to the emphasis given to recreation and to the Forest Service effort to compete with, and outdo, the National Park Service as a recreational entity. A new leadership philosophy is needed.[44]

By commending this view to the task force chairman, Colson appeared to be granting White House approval to the timber industry's cause.

Ten days later, the Forest Service responded to the industry–White House initiative by unveiling its FARR plan for increasing timber cutting. In effect, the plan proposed implementing the National Timber Supply Act—despite Congress. At an April 28, 1970, meeting, the task force's working group endorsed the industry–White House stratagem and the Forest Service's tactical plan. Afterward, the Forest Service member of the working group reported that there had been

> general agreement that while a bill is a desirable adjunct, it is not a necessity—[the Forest Service] can do everything it provides except establish "the fund." Also there seemed to be general agreement that a reasonable next step was presentation of the slightly revised Task Force report, along with a proposed Executive Memo directing the affected Secretaries to proceed to implement . . . the Task Force report.[45]

The President thereupon issued a statement and the Forest Service officially adopted its FARR plan. On June 19, 1970, President Nixon publicly endorsed the task force report. He declared: "The Secretaries of Agriculture and Interior should formulate plans to improve the level and quality of management of forest lands under their judisdiction in order to permit increased harvest of softwood timber consistent with sustained yield, environmental quality, and multiple use objectives." The President simultaneously released the report of the task force. Not surprisingly, it had recommended:

The Forest Service should be encouraged to push ahead with the development and implementation of programs to increase timber yields from the national forests. A goal of about 7 billion board foot annual increase in timber harvest from the national forests by 1978 is believed to be attainable and consistent with other objectives of forest management.[46]

President Nixon's pronouncement shocked Representative John P. Saylor (Pennsylvania), the ranking Republican on the House Interior Committee and a principal architect of the defeat, four months earlier, of the National Timber Supply Act. In an open letter to his fellow House members on June 23, 1970, he complained:

The effect of President Nixon's "directions" to the Agriculture, Housing and Interior Secretaries was to do by executive fiat what could not be done legislatively.

The Congress, in refusing to debate the infamous Timber Supply Act, maintained our national policy of protecting the public forests from the ravages of the timber cutting industry as previously established by the Multiple Use-Sustained Yield Act of 1960.

The lumber interests wanted this reasonable policy scrapped entirely. Failing with Congress, the lumber lobbyists went to the White House for help. The President's press conference was the result.[47]

Notwithstanding the protests of Congressman Saylor and the conservationists, the Forest Service proceeded to implement President Nixon's directive. In September 1970, it published its FARR plan under the popularized title of "A Forest Service Environmental Program for the 1970's." [48] Although, as noted earlier, the Forest Service is currently revising the program, its officials are ready to intensify the management, and increase the timber harvest, of the National Forests just as soon as the necessary funding is provided.

THE (NOT SO VERY) "ENVIRONMENTAL PROGRAM"

Implementation of the Environmental Program, or any of its recent intensified-management offshoots, would magnify the damage already being done to nontimber uses by timber harvesting. Most timber cutting disturbs recreation and wildlife habitat for a period of years. Clearcutting, faulty road construction, and delays in reforestation can cause erosion and water pollution serious enough to impair timber as well as nontimber uses for decades. Damage to forest lands and waters, in turn, limits their value for recreation. It also harms wildlife habitat and may reduce or disrupt water yield from forest watersheds.

Much Forest Service timber harvesting involves the lands recreationists find most appealing—the vast old-growth forests of the West, which have never been logged—Longfellow's "forest primeval." Here the stately, wonderfully proportioned Douglas-fir—two hundred to three hundred feet high and up to a thousand years old—holds unquestioned sway over a many-splendored kingdom. Along with the lesser pines, hemlocks, spruce, and an occasional patriarchal redwood, the fir shelters a rich, busy civilization of plants and animals. The bushes and wild flowers, silky mosses and delicate seedlings, the woodpeckers, grizzly bears, butterflies, and carefree salmon and trout coexist with a stunning beauty and equanimity.

A visit to an old-growth forest is a sensory delight. One can scramble up the side of a painted canyon, and gaze across a blanket of evergreens to cascading streams, clear blue lakes, and jagged, snowy peaks. Or one can sit on the spongy moss and pine needles of the valley floor, breathe in the moist fragrance of the enveloping forest, and watch the sunlight dart in and out of the trees as the wind gracefully parts the foliage far above. A visit to an old-growth forest is also a spiritual release for the tormented escapee of metropolis. As the late Bob Marshall, the revered onetime Forest Service Director of Recreation and founder of the Wilderness Society, said:

> For me and for thousands with similar inclinations, the most important passion of life is the overpowering desire to escape periodically from the clutches of a mechanistic civilization. To us the enjoyment of solitude, complete independence, and the beauty of undefiled panoramas is absolutely essential to happiness.[49]

Every year, the Forest Service carves roads and cuts timber on about one million acres of previously unroaded, unlogged National Forest land. That is the equivalent of annually cutting both Yosemite and Rocky Mountain National Parks, much of whose acreage is old-growth wilderness. About half of this annual harvest involves old-growth forests of pine and Douglas-fir.[50] Most of these forests the agency clearcuts. Under the FARR plan, the Forest Service will harvest an additional 201,000 acres of old-growth forests annually. This increase will further limit recreation and other nontimber uses of the National Forests. Forest users will not feel the full impact of the FARR plan, however, for sixty-nine years. At the end of that period, the massive, centuries-old Douglas-firs, dominating the picturesque valleys and mountainsides of the West, will be gone.

If, on the other hand, the Forest Service discards the FARR plan and continues cutting at present rates, it will liquidate the old-growth forests within ninety-three years.[51] In either case, the agency's timber cutting program will greatly affect nontimber uses of the most valuable National Forest lands. The Forest Service, however, has yet to recognize the multiple-use conflicts. In the version of the FARR plan released to the public, the Forest Service proposed to intensify all National Forest uses over the next ten years. At the same time, it fails to recognize the need for—and perhaps the impossibility of—coordinating increased timber production with other uses. Programs to build more campgrounds and seed more game habitat—however urgently needed—cannot offset the detriment to nontimber uses caused by accelerated timber cutting. According to Joseph F. Pechanec, a top Forest Service research official, the FARR plan's greatest defect is its failure to grasp the need to solve *current* management problems:

> The biggest deficiency may be that the [FARR] report talks blithely about the need for increased use and production from forests and ranges of many different kinds without seemingly recognizing that although there is a need to increase yields, the real basic problem is that the present level of management probably isn't adequate to sustain present levels of use. In other words, the fundamental problems are to improve the quality of land management and secondly to increase output.[52]

Not surprisingly, in arriving at the FARR cutting goals, the Forest Service virtually ignored constraints from nontimber values. The FARR task force determined the new cutting goals before even considering nontimber uses.

As early as March 12, 1969, an associate deputy chief of the Forest Service reported that an intensive management program would permit a 7.6-billion-board-foot annual increase in the allowable cut.[53] Since that figure exceeds the publicly announced goal of 7.4 billion board feet by only 0.2, it is clear that the Forest Service made no significant changes in the cutting target after March 12, 1969. But not until April 18, 1969, did the Forest Service leadership ask the directors of the Recreation, Wildlife Management, and other nontimber divisions to comment on the proposed increases in timber cutting.[54] Ten days later, the agency leadership went a step further. On April 28, 1969, it ordered the division directors to plan around the cutting goals, indicating that the goals were already firmly established:

> Your attention is called to the fact that the output targets for timber are set to meet the entire anticipated national need; i.e., balance the Nation's timber budget. Other targets do not; they are intended to display the portion of total national needs which the Forest Service can and should satisfy.[55]

The memorandum scarcely encouraged the nontimber divisions to point out conflicts. Nevertheless, upon receiving the initial draft FARR plan, many of the Forest Service officials responsible for nontimber forest uses objected strongly to the plan's neglect of multiple-use constraints. The Director of Forest Insect and Disease Research, for instance, noted on May 1, 1969, "I think there has crept into the statement, probably inadvertently, unnecessarily heavy emphasis on timber as the dominant consideration in resource management." [56]

A week later, the Assistant Director of Recreation protested to his division director, "I know we must give due attention to commodities, but I wish the [FARR] Task Force could find a way to keep timber from coming on so strong. Many groups and interests are apt to write us off as the same old timber-oriented outfit." [57] The same day, the Director of Recreation himself wrote:

> I cannot help getting the distinct feeling that the overriding thrust is meant to be directed toward maximizing timber production and that other resource considerations are meant to be tied to this only to the extent it can be done without in any way inpinging upon timber consideration and goals.[58]

The Forest Service's public relations officer criticized the explicit manner in which FARR had presented the cutting goals. "The proposed text is now overwhelmingly timber oriented . . ." he wrote on May 8, 1969.[59] The Director of Wildlife Management revealed his contempt for the FARR plan in a May 12, 1969, memorandum:

> Our greatest concern is over the repeated usage of the term "forests and related resources" [FARR]. If you mean "timber and related resources," then that terminology should be used. . . . Was it intended that the Appendix include only timber statistics? There is one chart on recreation, one on gross national product, and 28 on timber products.[60]

Even the Director of Timber Management admitted that "the assumptions used in developing a maximum effort lead to outputs that may be, in some cases, inconsistent with multiple use constraints. . . ."[61]

Important field officials also attacked the FARR plan. The Regional Forester for the Southwestern Region later wrote, "It is our opinion that the impacts on timber production from recreation and from maintaining natural beauty of the Forests were not adequately recognized."[62] And Joseph Pechanec, Director of the Intermountain Experiment Station, told then Deputy Chief John McGuire in early 1970:

> . . . knowing a substantial part of the West quite well and also knowing some of the fiction built into our inventory data, we wonder whether acceleration in management can actually meet the needs by 1980 and still provide for tradeoffs for improved environment, additional unroaded country in wilderness, and other demands on the land.[63]

In late October 1969, the Presidential Task Force on Softwood Lumber and Plywood called for increases of "7 to 8 billion board feet in annual timber harvest [on the National Forests] over the next decade."[64] Then Chief Cliff immediately dispelled any doubt that these goals reflected official Forest Service thinking. Referring to the task force document, he wrote the Assistant Secretary of Agriculture, on October 30, 1969, "This is a good report, and I believe the Secretary [of Agriculture] can approve it without any question."[65]

In his last three words, Chief Cliff in effect dismissed as irrelevant the very real questions raised by lower-ranking Forest Service officials five months before. Apparently he based his conclusion on nothing more than an ingrained belief that cutting increases, even as large as fifty percent, would not conflict with nontimber uses of the National Forests. The Nader Study Group specifically requested from the Chief the "documents, memoranda, or files which led you to conclude that such production increases were possible and consistent with multiple-use objectives." [66] Except for a 1968 study showing that the timber cutting goals were *biologically* attainable, the Forest Service was unable to produce a single substantiating document.[67]

Some Forest Service officials have been candid enough to admit that the FARR cutting increases were based on the assumption that maximum *sustainable* cutting rates were also *desirable,* even considering multiple-use impacts.[68] But the closest thing to an official acknowledgment that multiple-use constraints were ignored in setting the timber cutting goals was the statement in the Environmental Program report that

> Reaching this target level [7.4-billion-board-foot annual increase] will be dependent on . . . developing publicly acceptable timber harvesting and access practices which are compatible with scenic beauty, water quality, and other intangible environmental values.[69]

That is, techniques to make increased harvesting compatible with other uses do not yet exist, and will have to be developed. However, perhaps dangerously, the statement also implies that the Forest Service sees the conflict between timber cutting and nontimber uses as a public relations problem—getting the public to accept the higher cutting rates. William Lucas, chairman of the FARR task force, revealed this view in a September 1969 report. He acknowledged that the task force included in the plan proposals for increased spending on nontimber uses in an attempt to sell the timber goals to a potentially hostile public:

> It should be noted that the opportunity . . . to increase allowable cuts on the National Forests by investment in cultural practices possibly exists only over the

next decade. Acceleration of the cut in the old growth stands thereafter will probably be too rapid for the public to accept. Even now, questions are being raised about any acceleration of timber harvest. With a reasonable balance of acceleration in the watershed, wildlife, and scenic aspects of forest management, the FS [Forest Service] believes the increased production can be obtained without seriously upsetting the public.[70]

THE WILDERNESS CONTROVERSY

The enormous scope of Forest Service authority has drawn it into another environmental inferno—the debate over which National Forest lands, and how many, should be saved from all timber harvesting. The Forest Service pioneered the concept of protected wilderness when in 1924 it permanently banned all developmental activities, including timber production, on a 433,000-acre area of New Mexico's Gila National Forest. Over the next four decades, it officially set aside eighty-eight "Wilderness," "Wild," "Canoe," and "Primitive" Areas. Together they covered about 14.6 million acres, or 8 percent of the National Forest System.[71]

For many years conservationists applauded this far-sighted preservation policy. But as political and economic pressures in the 1950s and 1960s caused more and more undeveloped National Forest land to be logged, conservationists questioned whether mere administrative action offered adequate long-run protection of wilderness. After all, the agency that set aside these lands could just as easily return them to timber production at a later date. According to the Sierra Club, the Forest Service did reclassify between 1950 and 1964 about 800,000 acres of designated wilderness to permit timber cutting.[72] Timber industry spokesmen, meanwhile, attacked the administrative classification system because they feared the Forest Service would withdraw an excessive amount of land from the timber cutting base.[73]

With both views in mind, Congress passed the Wilderness Act in September 1964.[74] It afforded statutory protection as Wilderness Areas to 9.1 million acres of National Forest land to be preserved "untrammeled by man." It also directed the Secretary of Agriculture (through the Forest Service) to "study" within ten years an additional 5.5

million acres of administratively established National
Forest Primitive Areas for possible inclusion in the statutory Wilderness System. Finally, the Act reserved to Congress the ultimate decision on the establishment of these
additional areas and their boundaries.

   Both the Forest Service and Congress have taken an
inordinately long time to process and approve additions
to the Wilderness System. The Wilderness Act directed the
President to submit his "advice" to Congress on all Primitive Areas under study within ten years, and on two-thirds
of them within seven years, of its enactment. By January
1971, over six years after its enactment, the Forest Service
had completed hearings and developed recommendations
for only thirteen of the thirty-four primitive areas which it
was originally directed to study. These thirteen areas embraced only 1.2 million acres, or less than a quarter of the
5.5 million acres to be surveyed.[75] In late December 1971,
the Forest Service sent the President recommendations on
ten additional Primitive Areas. As a result, the President
exceeded by three months the statutory deadline of September 1971 for dispatching to Congress his own recommendations on two-thirds of the thirty-four areas under
study.[76] Partly as a result of the delays, Congress had
acted on only eleven of the twenty-three wilderness proposals (approving all eleven) by January 1973.

   The Forest Service has taken advantage of the delays to
try to build logging roads and sell timber along the borders
of several Primitive Areas under study. By changing the
character of the land, the agency can make it "unsuitable"
for wilderness classification. Only a federal court order
prevented the Forest Service in 1969 from logging wilderness lands adjacent to Colorado's Gore Range–Eagle Nest
Primitive Area.[77] The Forest Service also attempted to log
the Magruder Corridor, once part of Idaho's Selway-Bitter-
root Primitive Area. In 1963, over massive conservationist
protest, the Forest Service declassified the Corridor and
included it in timber management planning. Conservationists organized to stop the agency from logging the area.
After extensive hearings and review by the Secretary of
Agriculture, the Forest Service came up with a "compro-
mise" proposal to log only half of the area. All of it was
once Primitive Area and would have become part of a new
Wilderness Area.

To its credit, the Forest Service has added 482,000 acres to the twenty-three Primitive Areas it has recommended thus far for wilderness classification.[78] But to many areas the agency added far less acreage than conservationists asserted was necessary to maintain the integrity of the wilderness involved. Where the Forest Service limited proposed areas with new logging and road-building, it was usurping the authority to determine the boundaries of Wilderness Areas which Congress specifically reserved to itself.[79]

The Council on Environmental Quality became so concerned about Forest Service foot-dragging and "wilderness-preventive logging" that it drafted an Executive Order in April 1971.[80] The Order directed the Forest Service to identify within 120 days all de facto wilderness lands contiguous to Primitive Areas. It also directed the agency to protect these lands in their natural, undisturbed state until the President and Congress could complete a full review of their wilderness potential. CEQ never asked the President to sign the Order because it felt that the court ruling in the Colorado Primitive Area case accomplished its purpose.[81]

Debate also rages over the designation as Wilderness Areas of additional wild lands not now protected as Primitive Areas. According to the Forest Service the National Forests contain 1,448 unlogged, unroaded areas, each five thousand acres or larger. Together they cover 55.9 million acres—approximately the area of Ohio and Pennsylvania combined.[82] Some outdoor recreationists would like the Forest Service to ban timber cutting on a portion of these lands, preserving them for wilderness and mass-recreational development. In January 1972, the Sierra Club listed 10.2 million acres of de facto wildernesses in Washington, Oregon, Idaho, and Montana which, it said, contain some of the "most superb scenery" in the country. It urged the Forest Service to study them and recommended their inclusion in the Wilderness System.[83]

The timber industry vehemently opposes the creation of new Wilderness Areas from lands outside existing Primitive Areas. It makes no sense to industry spokesmen to let timber go unmanaged and unused. As the executive vice-president of the Appalachian Hardwood Manufacturers, Inc., told a Senate subcommittee last year:

> The preserves that we see in our forests today are
> graveyards of once fine trees, now rotting hulks on the
> forest floor, sent into oblivion by the sincere, but mis-
> guided efforts of those who would confuse preserva-
> tion with conservation.[84]

The industry fears that Congress will "lock up" huge
amounts of live timber in new Wilderness Areas, thus
preventing its use of the timber and its conversion into
profit.

In fact, however, existing and proposed Wilderness
Areas do not contain sizable quantities of timber. Less than
five percent of the sawtimber inventory and ten percent of
the land in the National Forests of the eleven westernmost
states is "locked up" in Wilderness and Primitive Areas.[85]
None of the three small Wilderness Areas in the eastern
United States includes valuable sawtimber. Moreover, the
10.2 million acres of National Forest land in the Pacific
Northwest which the Sierra Club has recommended for
wilderness classification contain only 1.2 percent of the
National Forest timber available for cutting in that region.[86]

Although long a promoter of wilderness preservation, the
Forest Service has responded sluggishly to conservationists'
proposals for additional protected areas. In the late 1950s,
for instance, the Forest Service reluctantly acceded to public demands for a Glacier Peak Wilderness Area in the
Cascade Range of Washington State. But to permit future
logging of the scenic, heavily timbered valleys nearby, the
Forest Service limited the reservation chiefly to rocky alpine
areas. Conservationists angrily dubbed the proposal the
"Wilderness on the Rocks." According to Brock Evans, then
Northwest representative of the Sierra Club:

> It took a series of bitter hearings and enormous pub-
> lic pressure to force the Forest Service to include even
> a part of the disputed low-elevation valleys, which were
> also an integral part of the wilderness.[87]

When the Forest Service continued to log adjacent wild
areas, Northwest conservationists appealed to Congress for
help. In 1968, Congress responded by creating the North
Cascades National Park—thus withdrawing the disputed
wilderness lands from Forest Service jurisdiction, and
timber cutting.

Several years ago, conservationists urged protection of

a splendid 700,000-acre wilderness adjoining Glacier National Park in Montana's Flathead National Forest. Shortly thereafter, the Forest Service began penetrating the wilderness with a logging road, purportedly to open up the area for "multiple use." The conservationists saw the move as an attempt to prevent the area from being classified as wilderness. Indeed, John L. Hall, district ranger during the years when the roads were planned, has admitted as much to the Sierra Club's Brock Evans. Now special assistant to the Alaskan regional forester, Hall told Evans several years ago that "this was the deliberate intent—to ring the area with roads so that it could not be added to the Bob Marshall Wilderness to the south." [88]

The Wilderness Act of 1964 did not require the Forest Service to study and recommend preservation of wildernesses other than those adjoining Primitive Areas.* At the urging of wilderness proponents, however, the Forest Service launched a survey in January 1967 to locate potential new areas. The Chief ordered the regional foresters to map all roadless, undeveloped areas of five thousand acres or more under their jurisdictions, and to recommend certain of these areas for study and possible wilderness designation.[90] Since the agency plans to protect *only* the recommended areas from roading and logging, their selection constitutes the crucial step in the classification of additional Wilderness Areas.

Conservationists hopefully assumed that the regional foresters would employ the Wilderness Act's criteria in selecting "New Wilderness Study Areas." The Act defines wilderness as "an area of undeveloped Federal land retaining its primeval character . . . without permanent improvements or human habitation . . . with the imprint of man's work substantially unnoticeable.[91] But the Chief had in mind narrower criteria—"the tests of suitability, availability, and need." [92]

To recommend a potential wilderness area just for study, the regional forester had to judge it "available" and "needed" considering alternative uses of the land—

---

* Nevertheless, the Act did require the Secretary of *Interior* to review "every roadless area of five thousand contiguous acres or more" in National Parks, National Wildlife Refuges, and other lands under his jurisdiction, and to "report to the President his recommendations as to the suitability or nonsuitability of each such area or island for preservation as wilderness." [89]

especially timber production. "Suitability," in terms of its wilderness character, was no longer sufficient. Few areas containing valuable timber—which is a large portion of National Forest roadless acreage—can pass such stiff, output-oriented tests. Fewer still will survive the intensive study to be undertaken by the Forest Service from 1974 to 1984 prior to recommending new areas to Congress. The pressure from Washington to increase timber production will be too great.

The regional foresters postponed action on the Chief's directive through the politically volatile timber supply crisis, 1968 to 1970. Their procrastination led the President's Council on Environmental Quality (CEQ) to draft in early 1971 a stern Executive Order to expedite the review.[93] It was never issued, partly because in February 1971 the Chief of the Forest Service ordered the regional foresters to act.[94] By August, the review was under way. Ten months later, the foresters offered their recommendations to the Chief. In January 1973, Chief John R. McGuire released a proposed list of 235 New Wilderness Study Areas, encompassing 11 million acres in fourteen states and Puerto Rico. Almost a quarter of the total acreage is in Alaska, most of whose forest lands cannot produce timber economically in any case. Only three areas, embracing 45,000 acres, lie east of the Rocky Mountains. New Study Areas in Idaho, Montana, Oregon, and Washington—leading timber-producing states—cover only 3.7 million acres; the Sierra Club had urged preservation of 10.2 million acres in these four states. Preservation of all the New Study Areas would diminish the allowable cut of the National Forest by only two percent. Setting aside all 55.9 million acres of roadless areas—only 18.6 million of which are classified as "commercial [productive] forest land"—would reduce the annual allowable cut by 20 percent.[95]

Ironically, after holding back for years, the Forest Service conducted the survey perhaps too expeditiously. The Chief's criteria seemed to demand extensive—and, by necessity, time-consuming—investigation. A complete, accurate review would require studies of climate, topography, soils, water quality, fish and wildlife, potential uses of the area, economic factors, demographic patterns, recreation use and demand in the region, and transportation trends. Many of these studies will be components of the Forest

Service's ongoing multiple-use inventory. By Forest Service estimate, however, the inventory will take at least ten *years* to complete.[96] The ten *months* allotted to identifying New Study Areas could hardly have allowed for such complex surveys and analyses. Just the timing of the wilderness review, in fact, reduced its accuracy. From late fall until spring or early summer, snow covers most of the de facto wilderness areas, thus hindering access to, let alone thorough examination of, the areas.

Moreover, despite its new emphasis on public involvement, the Forest Service offered members of the public very little time to comment on its initial Study Area selections. Seven of the nine regional foresters allowed the public only a few weeks to examine and comment on their tentative selections. William J. Lucas,* Rocky Mountain regional forester, refused to release his tentative selections, thus preventing *any* public participation. C. A. Yates, Alaskan regional forester, ignored the entire wilderness review. Having completed the region's new multiple-use inventory and recommended several wilderness Study Areas prior to the review, he refrained from reexamining region lands for additional recommendations.[97]

Citing these factors and the arbitrary procedures employed by several regional foresters, four conservation groups filed suit in federal court, June 16, 1972, to freeze the wilderness review. The Sierra Club, the Natural Resources Defense Council, and two other groups asked for a permanent injunction preventing the Forest Service from disturbing the 55.9 million acres of roadless areas until it had thoroughly studied, with a "fair opportunity for public participation," all of them for possible designation as New Study Areas.[98] In effect, the groups were asking the court to order the Forest Service to implement the CEQ's draft Executive Order.

Two weeks later the groups obtained a temporary restraining order, and in August a preliminary injunction, protecting the roadless areas from development during litigation. Before trial, scheduled for December, the Forest Service agreed to file with the CEQ formal Environmental Impact Statements before authorizing any future contracts

---

* Before becoming Rocky Mountain regional forester, Lucas was chairman of the FARR task force, which developed the Forest Service's accelerated cutting goals for the next decade.

for development of the 1,213 roadless areas not designated New Wilderness Study Areas. Noting this concession, the trial court dismissed the suit "without prejudice"—that is, permitting the conservationists to sue again on the same issue.[99]

The Sierra Club suit, which annoyed the Forest Service and panicked the timber industry,[100] forced onto a national forum an issue with truly national ramifications which the Forest Service had been sitting on for too long. That issue extends beyond the identification and protection of additional Wilderness Areas. It involves the determination of how much timber cutting is desirable and on which public lands. Congress would provide a far more equitable national forum for its solution than the federal courts. But perhaps the expected stream of court suits is necessary to goad Congress into establishing more precise National Forest management standards. In any case, the Forest Service should never have presumed it had the authority to make national policy. However noble its intentions, it should not have attempted a hasty, incomplete review of roadless areas. Instead, it should have asked Congress to clarify its original policy directive on wilderness—the Wilderness Act of 1964.

Congress is now considering a related policy issue which the Forest Service similarly tried and failed to resolve on its own. Several bills, if enacted, would designate additional wilderness areas in the eastern United States. Despite their tremendous population and growing need for recreation land, the states east of the Rocky Mountains now contain only three designated Wilderness Areas (and no Primitive Areas). Although many western Wilderness Areas exceed 100,000 acres, none of the eastern areas is over 15,000 acres. The eastern National Forests cover 23 million acres scattered through twenty-five states.

Except for the three New Study Areas in North Carolina, Florida, and Puerto Rico, the Forest Service has resisted the establishment of additional areas in the East. It contends that proposed eastern areas are not "pure" enough for wilderness classification. Most National Forest lands in the East were once logged or roaded, although often so long ago that they now exhibit few traces of development. Nevertheless, the Forest Service argues that the Wilderness Act excludes these areas because they are not "undeveloped

Federal land retaining its primeval character and influence. . . .[101]

Chief McGuire explained the Forest Service's position at Senate hearings in February 1973:

> If almost any of the restored eastern National Forest lands . . . were deemed to meet present Wilderness Act criteria, it would be extremely difficult to define a degree of disturbance that would disqualify many millions of acres of Federal lands for wilderness consideration.[102]

In other words, he seemed to be saying, the Forest Service would be compelled to withdraw from timber harvesting and other uses a large portion of the National Forests in the West as well as the East. Second, the Chief warned, "stretching" the definition of wilderness in the Act would result in the lowering of wilderness *management* standards—"which might allow wilderness opponents to demand more intensive use of existing Wilderness Areas." [103]

Conservationists do not share Chief McGuire's anxieties. They point out that the Wilderness Act's definition contains a clause which sanctions the designation of once-developed lands as Wilderness. The Act declares that a Wilderness Area is one which "generally appears to have been affected primarily [not 'solely'] by the forces of nature, with the imprint of man's work substantially unnoticeable [not 'wholly absent']." [104] As Senator Frank Church (Democrat of Idaho), a senior member of the Senate Interior Committee, said at hearings in May 1972:

> I have heard it said by some who are simply illinformed that no areas in the eastern United States can meet the test of qualification under the definition of wilderness in the Wilderness Act. That is just not so. Indeed, we placed three national forest wilderness units into the National Wilderness Preservation System in the 1964 act, all of which lie in the East, all of which had a former history of some land abuse. . . . There are other areas in the eastern national forests which will certainly be found to be suitable, if the Forest Service will approach its task and obligations in a reasonable and responsive manner.[105]

Second, since the Wilderness Act leaves in the discretion of Congress how much wilderness to preserve, the inclusion in the Wilderness System of *some* restored public lands will not automatically force the withdrawal from timber production of *all* such lands. Finally, the Act clearly distinguishes between the criteria for selecting new Wilderness Areas and the criteria for managing them once they have been selected; [106] the Forest Service's fear that "stretching" the former will lead to loosening the latter is without foundation.

At this writing, the Forest Service and the conservationists are battling the issue in Congress. The conservationists are pushing a bill declaring that restored wildernesses conform to the Wilderness Act's definition. Sponsored by Senator Henry M. Jackson (Democrat of Washington) and Representative James A. Haley (Democrat of Florida), the chairmen of the Senate and House Interior Committees, the bill would immediately designate as Wilderness Areas twenty-eight National Forest tracts covering some 471,000 acres in sixteen eastern states.[107] The Forest Service is countering with legislation amending the Wilderness Act to include a separate, broader definition of wilderness to be applied only to restored National Forest lands east of the 100th meridian. Its bill would designate no Wilderness Areas immediately, but would merely direct the Forest Service to review fifty-three eastern areas for possible designation.[108]

Meanwhile, the Senate Agriculture and Forestry Committee has reported to the full Senate a bill establishing a National Forest Wild Areas System. Distinct from the Wilderness System, it would eventually comprise all eastern wildernesses meeting the Forest Service's revised criteria for restored lands. A leading conservation lobbyist, George Alderson, sees the Agriculture Committee's move as an assertion of more authority over the National Forests:

> But why? We can only speculate: Probably to build a little more power for the committee, possibly even to head off the Interior Committee's venture into forest management issues which resulted in the death last year of the timber industry's bill to allow more logging on federal lands.[109]

Conservationists also suspect the Forest Service of working behind the scenes for the Wild Areas bill in order to limit the number of wildernesses eventually established by Congress. Alderson observed in March 1973:

> The Forest Service's objective on Capitol Hill is evidently to get its eastern lands firmly away from the Interior Committee, where citizens have a great deal of influence, and let the Agriculture Committee do the dirty work of turning down all the wilderness or wild area proposals.[110]

If the Wild Areas bill becomes law, the sponsoring committee—the Agriculture Committee—would, under Senate rules, have jurisdiction over subsequent legislative proposals for new wild areas. The Interior Committee sponsored the Wilderness Act of 1964; consequently, it now has jurisdiction over new Wilderness Area bills.

Except for infrequently establishing National Parks, Congress has never considered banning timber cutting on National Forest land to permit *intensive* recreation. Timber industry spokesmen tend to polarize the issue by maintaining that the only alternative to timber cutting is to lock up the forest for the "few Sierra Club types" who want absolute wilderness. They point out that most Americans do not enjoy hiking miles into Wilderness Areas "untrammeled by man." According to chief timber lobbyist Ralph D. Hodges, Jr., "Most people don't know the difference between wilderness and multiple use lands." [111] Skiers, cyclists, campers, snowmobile enthusiasts, and car-bound sightseers care little about the breathtaking vistas obtainable only after miles of rugged backpacking.

The Forest Service, in turn, argues that *all* National Forest lands are available for recreation under multiple-use management. If an especially scenic area requires protection, it adds, the agency already has the authority to protect the area from cutting. But multiple-use management, which sanctions timber cutting and livestock grazing, can easily mar the beauty of a near-wild area which snowmobilers, bicyclists, or automobile campers might otherwise enjoy. Moreover, other than Wilderness and Primitive Areas, the Forest Service has actually protected for recreation less than 1 percent of all National Forest lands— 786,576 acres.[112]

Eventually, Congress will have to resolve this policy issue as it will the many problems surrounding the Forest Service's current wilderness review. If it does not, the Forest Service may find itself ensnarled in yet another crippling controversy.

5

"Bureaucracy Running Wild"

🌲 🌲

Professional planners and managers cannot be dispensed with. But some means of public participation, however inadequate, would at least offer the beginning of a system of planning that would encompass a broader vision and a deeper relation to democratic ideals. For the experts and professionals have their limitations. They can tell us whether an area of forest can be lumbered at a commercially feasible price. But can they tell us whether an "overmature, spike-topped, catfaced, conky old veteran" should be saved for future generations? [1]
Professor Charles A. Reich
Yale Law School, 1962

Why, after promoting wilderness preservation for decades, has the Forest Service turned sour to the idea? "The bulk of Forest Service people have never fully embraced wilderness," Thurman Trosper, president of the Wilderness Society and formerly a National Forest supervisor, explains. The more compelling reason may be that Forest Service officials, even those who strongly advocate wilderness preservation, "don't want [Congress] to curtail their discretion." It took the personal intervention of President Kennedy, Trosper recalls, to reverse the Forest Service's opposition to the original Wilderness Bill.[2]

From the time it received its expansive mandate to administer the National Forests "for the permanent good of the whole people," the Forest Service has guarded its independence jealously. With the exception of the Wilderness Act of 1964, Congress has never significantly limited the Service's power to legislate National Forest policy. Like most federal agencies, the Forest Service has lost, and partially forfeited, some of its discretion to a budget-manipulating White House. But in the day-to-day manage-ment of the National Forests, it reigns supreme. Although it has responded affirmatively to a number of citizen complaints, it steadfastly refuses to admit the public into its decision-making process.

I.   An (Almost) Independent Agency

The Forest Service owes much of its independence to its anomalous location in the Department of Agriculture. Prior to 1905, the National Forests were administered by the Department of the Interior, which then, as now, managed most federal lands. Fearing that corrupt Interior Department officials might sacrifice the valuable forests to powerful land and logging interests, President Theodore Roosevelt persuaded Congress to place the nascent Forest Service in the Department of Agriculture.

Today, although vested with exclusive National Forest management powers, the Secretary of Agriculture exercises little control over his department's biggest agency. The Forest Service deals directly with Congress, for instance. At committee hearings on forestry legislation, an Assistant Secretary of Agriculture usually makes a pro forma opening statement, but the Forest Service drafts it, and the Chief of the Forest Service offers detailed testimony. If the Chief takes issue with the Administration's position on a bill, the committee members—alerted to his misgivings through informal staff contacts—have no trouble eliciting his views. In 1973, for instance, the Forest Service was stunned by Presidential cutbacks in its FY 1974 budget. Testifying before the Senate Appropriations Committee in favor of an Administration-approved budget of $457 million, Chief John R. McGuire readily admitted that the Forest Service needed, and had originally requested of the Administration, almost twice that amount.[3]

The Agriculture Department also has little say in the selection of top Forest Service personnel. Traditionally, the Secretary of Agriculture appoints only the Chief of the Forest Service; the Chief appoints his subordinates. Moreover, "because of the professional nature of the job," [4] chiefs have always been appointed from the senior ranks of the Forest Service itself and have served, not at the pleasure of the Secretary or the President, but up to retirement age. For example, Edward P. Cliff retired as Chief on April 30, 1972, after serving as head of the Forest Service for ten years and as an employee for forty-one. His successor, John R. McGuire, a Forest Service employee since the 1940s, merely moved up from Associate Chief, the agency's number-two position.

The Forest Service's independent course has moved frustrated Cabinet Secretaries, Presidents, and others to urge its transfer to the Interior Department. Harold L. Ickes, Franklin Roosevelt's Secretary of the Interior, fought hard for a transfer, accusing the Forest Service of being "a tight little organization that does a lot of lobbying . . . an example of bureaucracy running wild even to the extent of defying the express orders of the President and opposing a bill which was introduced with his knowledge and consent." Only Pearl Harbor and a vigorous counterattack by the aging Gifford Pinchot and other foresters kept President Roosevelt from signing a transfer order.[5]

More recently, members of Congress and President Nixon proposed making the Forest Service part of a new Department of Natural Resources, arguing that it belongs in the same department with other federal land management agencies.[6] Some conservationists support President Nixon's reorganization plan as a way to tame the Forest Service, which they feel has abused its autonomy. It is questionable, however, whether a Department of Natural Resources would have any better luck than the Department of Agriculture. A new department, managing all federal lands and coordinating the functions of the Forest Service and other agencies, might reduce the power of any one of them. But, unless a Secretary of Natural Resources exercised control over the Forest Service's personnel system and severed its strong links to Congress, his attempts to master the agency would fail.

Other conservationists argue that the way to improve conditions in the National Forests is not to place their management in the hands of officials likely to multiply past environmental blunders. The management philosophy of a Department of Natural Resources, they contend, will naturally reflect that of its principal agencies—the Bureau of Land Management, the Bureau of Mines, the Bureau of Reclamation, and the Atomic Energy Commission. It will therefore emphasize resource exploitation over resource conservation, ecosystem protection, and outdoor recreation. To place the Forest Service in such a department would be to destroy whatever remains of multiple-use management. These conservationists propose instead the establishment of a Department of Conservation, with the Forest Service as its core. The new department might also include the National Park Service, the Bureau of Sport Fisheries and Wildlife, the Bureau of Outdoor Recreation, and the recreational land management functions of the Bureau of Reclamation and the Army Corps of Engineers. The department's management philosophy, according to its proponents, would be to protect and conserve natural resources for wilderness and limited use, especially recreation.

AXING THE FOREST SERVICE BUDGET

An agency's ability to chart an independent course is largely determined by its power to spend freely within its overall budget. By modifying Forest Service budget requests for specific programs, the Agriculture Department and the Bureau of the Budget or its successor, the President's Office of Management and Budget (OMB), have obtained a degree of control over Forest Service activities which many thought impossible without major executive reorganization. Ironically, this budgetary offensive is sabotaging the Forest Service's own belated attempts to banish an unfortunate product of its autonomy—its protimber bias.

Each year, the Chief of the Forest Service asks his division directors and field officials for estimates of their funding needs for the coming fiscal year. Observing the ceiling set for the agency by the Department of Agriculture (on the basis of OMB guidelines), the Chief adjusts and combines the estimates into a single Forest Service budget request. Before being submitted to Congress, the request must stand trial before the Agriculture Department and the OMB. Almost as a matter of course, the department reduces the Forest Service's proposal by ten to fifteen percent. The OMB, which has the authority to ease or rescind the department's action, regularly slices off an additional ten percent. For FY 1974, the department and the OMB were especially severe, lopping forty-six percent off the Forest Service's request.[7]

Every administrative agency must expect higher budgetary authorities to trim its requests. What Forest Service officials, Congressmen, and conservationists find objectionable in the Forest Service cutbacks is not so much their severity as their selectivity. Commodity programs, such as timber production, cattle grazing, and mining, are generously funded; noncommodity programs, such as recreation, watershed, and wildlife habitat, are not.* Over the period FY 1962–FY 1972, for instance, the department's budget requests for timber sales administration averaged 99 percent of the Forest Service requests, and for range resource management, 93 percent. OMB (formerly Budget Bureau) requests for the same items averaged 92 percent and 87 percent, respectively. For the noncommodity programs of wildlife habitat management, recreation-public use, reforestation, and forest research, however, the department's requests averaged only 89 percent, 87 percent, 82 percent, and 78 percent, respectively, of Forest Service requests. OMB cutbacks were even more dramatic. Its requests for the same four items averaged 79 percent, 72 percent, 67 percent, and 66 percent of original Forest Service proposals.

Moreover, the OMB does not sheathe its budgetary knife when it forwards the President's budget to Congress. *After* Congress acts, the OMB frequently "places in reserve" some of the appropriated funds. In fiscal year 1973, the OMB impounded $54 million of total Forest Service appropriations of $562 million.[8] Although most budget items were affected, the noncommodity items were hit especially hard. Reforestation appropriations were reduced by 8 percent. Funding for wildlife management research and construction of facilities for public recreation, water resource development, and research was more than cut in half. Financing of a program to develop less environmentally destructive logging techniques was completely wiped out. Not surprisingly, commodity items fared considerably better. The OMB impounded only about one percent of timber sales administration appropriations, and less than four percent of timber management research, forest products research, and forest resource economics research appropriations.

At budget hearings, Congress appears receptive to the

* See Appendix 5-1, "Forest Service Budget Estimates and Appropriations, Fiscal Years 1955–1972."

full-funding pleas of foresters, conservationists, and Forest Service officials. But when it comes to voting, Congress invariably adopts the shriveled OMB version of the Forest Service budget. Over the period 1962 to 1972, OMB requests averaged 77 percent of Forest Service requests; Congressional appropriations, 80 percent. Like the OMB requests, appropriations fattened commodity uses and starved noncommodity uses. Appropriations for timber sales administration, for instance, averaged 96 percent of Forest Service requests. Appropriations for recreation-public use, on the other hand, averaged 72 percent of Forest Service requests.

In favoring commodity programs, the OMB could merely be falling for the timber industry's spurious rationale for accelerated National Forest timber cutting. The relationship between the Nixon Administration and the timber and home-building industries no doubt sweetens this logic. Frederick L. Webber, former vice-president of the American Paper Institute, joined the White House staff in mid-1973 as Special Assistant to the President for Legislative Affairs. E. F. Behrens, a former executive of the National Forest Products Association, holds a similar legislative liaison post in the Department of Agriculture. In the first Nixon Administration, Eugene A. Gulledge, a one-time officer of the National Association of Home-Builders, was an Assistant Secretary of Housing and Urban Development.

An incident during the industries' campaign to increase National Forest timber cutting through the abortive National Timber Supply Act of 1969 illustrates the coziness of industry–White House relations. Despairing at the Forest Service's endorsement of the bill, a prominent Washington conservationist telephoned then Presidential adviser Charles W. Colson for help in blocking the legislation. Colson was in conference, but his secretary offered to help. When the conservationist mentioned the timber supply bill, she replied: "Oh, you'll have to talk to Ralph Hodges about that. He's handling all the timber matters for us. I'll give you his number." [9] Hodges is executive vice-president of the National Forest Products Association.

Congress follows the OMB's lead in slanting the Forest Service budget toward timber production partly because that activity earns money for the government and electoral

support for Congressmen. The sale of National Forest timber returns millions of dollars every year to the U.S. Treasury–in FY 1973, an estimated $398 million.[10] Bigger appro-
priations for timber sales administration mean additional
millions in federal income. Most nontimber activities, on
the other hand, cost the Treasury money.

Moreover, as noted in Chapter 2, promotion of National
Forest timber production yields political dividends. Many
residents of western states make their living in timber-
related industries, which in turn depend to some extent on
National Forest timber. They also receive generous public
service benefits from National Forest timber cutting. In
lieu of taxes, the federal government pays to counties containing tax-exempt National Forest land 25 percent of the
receipts from National Forest timber sales within their
bounds. The funds are earmarked for school and highway
construction. Another 10 percent of the timber sales receipts are spent on construction and maintenance of National Forest roads and trails in the states producing the
revenues.[11] Higher employment and larger federal rebates
resulting from increased cutting in the National Forests
translate into electoral support for Congressmen from
timber-producing areas. When the cutting slackens, so does
the support.

A decade of Presidential and Congressional emphasis on
timber production has given the Forest Service budget the
look of a logging company's financial statement. The Multiple Use–Sustained Yield Act of 1960 declare that "the national forests are established and shall be administered
for outdoor recreation, range, timber, watershed, and wildlife and fish purposes." [12] In lobbying for passage of the
Act, then Forest Service Chief Richard McArdle called on
Congress to make it "abundantly clear either in the statute
itself or in the legislative history that the [five] *resources
will be given equal consideration* in general and over the
national forest system as a whole" [emphasis added].[13]
Today's Forest Service budget of $562 million—two-thirds
of which funds activities associated with timber production
—mocks Chief McArdle's dedication to "equal consideration." *

* See Appendix 5-2, "Forest Service Appropriations, FY 1973."

In fiscal year 1973, Congress appropriated $99.8 million for timber resource management. The Forest Service used two-thirds of this money to administer timber sales and supervise timber cutting in the National Forests. The remaining third was spent reforesting harvested areas and thinning middle-aged timber stands to achieve faster growth. Forest roads and trails usually receive a larger appropriation than any other item in the budget—$158.8 million in FY 1973. Most of this appropriation finances construction and maintenance of roads used initially for logging and subsequently for fire protection, thinning and timber stand improvement, recreation, and other activities. In FY 1973, Congress also allotted $54.7 million to forest fire and pest control and $32.8 million to state and private forest management assistance. These appropriations chiefly benefited timber production. Finally, $48.6 million of the $61.1 million appropriated for forest research went to timber management, protection, product utilization, and marketing research. Altogether, of regular Forest Service appropriations for FY 1973 of $561.8 million, $394.7 million funded programs relating to timber production.

Nontimber management activities, on the other hand, received a mere $167.1 million—less than a third of total appropriations. Only $41.4 million, a tenth of the total Forest Service budget, went to recreation–public use for construction and maintenance of campgrounds, scenic areas, and other visitor facilities. It also financed the administration of National Recreation Areas, Wilderness Areas, Trails, Wild and Scenic Rivers, and other Congressionally protected areas managed by the Forest Service. These areas and facilities must serve a recreational public which in 1973 spent close to 200 million visitor-days in the National Forests.

The Forest Service budget also devotes little money to management for other nontimber uses. Congress appropriated $9.7 million for soil and water management. This small allocation must cover protection of forty million acres of National Forest watershed, geological and hydrological surveys, monitoring the effects of timber harvesting on soil and water, and restoring eroded lands and polluted streams. Congress appropriated $7.7 million for wildlife habitat management. Under this item, the Forest Service funds

coordination of timber activities with the biological needs
of forest wildlife, enhancement of fish and game habitat,
and protection of rare species. For the acquisition of private
lands within National Forest boundaries, Congress appropriated a minuscule $1.3 million for FY 1973.* Finally, a
mere $12.5 million went to research not connected with
timber production.

Because its budget has long favored timber management,
the Forest Service has failed to take the management measures for nontimber uses which its planners called for ten
years ago. In September 1961, President Kennedy sent to
Congress a ten-year "Development Program for the National Forests," drafted by the Forest Service.[15] It charted
intensified management of all renewable resources in the
National Forests for fiscal years 1963 through 1972. By
the end of the plan period, timber sales administration had
received 98.9 percent of scheduled funding.† Insect and
disease control, forest roads and trails, and forest fire protection—all contributing chiefly to timber production—
had been funded at 89.5, 78.6, and 69.7 percent of their
respective projected levels. Other commodity uses, such as
range resource management and mineral claims, leases,
and special uses, had received at least three-quarters of
planned financing.

On the other hand, reforestation—the victim of the
budgeteers' "cut now, plant later" philosophy—had received
by FY 1973 only 41.5 percent of projected funding. Noncommodity uses have been underfinanced perpetually. Even
though recreation use of the National Forests has sky-
rocketed to the level predicted by the 1962 program, funding for recreation–public use has lagged far behind. By the
end of the ten-year plan period, it stood at 44.0 percent of
its scheduled amount. As a result, the Forest Service's program to construct and maintain campsites, picnic grounds,
and visitor facilities has failed to keep pace with recreation
demand. By the end of FY 1972, wildlife habitat management, always starved for funds, had been financed at only

* Under the Land and Water Conservation Fund Act of 1965,[14] Congress appropriated $29.7 million for Forest Service acquisition of
recreational lands.
† See Appendix 5-3, "Status of Financing Development Program for
the National Forests."

61.1 percent of its planned level. Consequently, fewer fish and animal species—some near extinction and many valuable for sport fishing and hunting—have benefited from Forest Service efforts to protect and enhance their habitat. Finally, acquisition of lands had received only 24.4 percent of its projected funding by the plan's tenth year. Thus, despite its purchase of forest lands for recreation under the Land and Water Conservation Fund Act, the Forest Service has failed to acquire most of the 950,000 acres of privately owned land within National Forest boundaries needed for other purposes.

(By twisting and chopping Forest Service budget requests, the timber-hungry OMB and Congressional Appropriations Committees are frustrating Forest Service efforts to eliminate its timber production bias. To some extent, the Forest Service painted itself into a corner. In hopes of obtaining more money for nontimber functions, it tried year after year to entice the OMB and Congress to expand its entire budget by requesting ever larger appropriations for its politically popular timber activities. But its failure to back up nontimber requests with the solid cost-effectiveness reasoning accompanying its timber requests doomed the strategy. The OMB and Congress enthusiastically granted the requested budget increases for timber functions, while largely ignoring those for nontimber functions.

Some Forest Service officials have faulted the agency for not estimating accurately the cost of genuine multiple-use management and for not lobbying aggressively with the OMB and Congress to obtain the necessary funds.[16] Economist Richard M. Alston, a consultant to the Forest Service, attributes the agency's difficulty in achieving a funding balance to its failure to justify nontimber budget requests in terms of clearly specified programs and goals:

> If budget requests are tied directly to explicit program and project planning, the agency will be able to support them as actual needs to carry out the mandate of the legislation. This can only be done if the agency forthrightly adopts a goal-oriented, management decision-making program and works directly to improve its capability to demonstrate the costs and consequences of alternative management programs, projects, and activities. If the "priority juggling" evident

in the budget data is to stop, the Congress, the Office of Management and Budget, and the Department of Agriculture must be shown the reasoning behind the Forest Service budget requests and the evidence to support it.[17]

If and when goal-oriented management becomes a reality, Alston says, the Department of Agriculture and the OMB should alter only the total size of the Forest Service budget. If the two wish to meddle with specific Forest Service program requests, "they should use the means available to them to secure changes in the legislative mandate that determines the budget requests." Congress, under Alston's model, would alter Forest Service-requested funding levels only in response to statutory changes in the agency's mandate or "as an indication that new or different priorities are being established on behalf of the public."

Few political scientists, or Forest Service officials, could quarrel with Alston's logic. Nevertheless, it exhibits several possibly crippling flaws. As Alston himself says, "It [his model] is admittedly idealistic in that it does not take into account the realities of politics." The OMB, which under President Nixon has developed immense supervisory powers over the federal bureaucracy, will not soon abandon its practice of amending specific Forest Service program requests—goal-oriented planning or no. And without new, priority-setting statutes to guide them, the Congressional appropriations committees will not soon begin rejecting the OMB's timber-based recommendations. Moreover, as we will discuss later, the Forest Service itself cannot adequately rationalize its management planning and budget requests until Congress and the general public clarify its mandate.

II. Forest Service Decision-Making: No Trespassing

Budget manipulation by the OMB and Congress has not diminished the Forest Service's power to *spend* appropriated funds as it alone thinks best. Delegated broad powers by Congress, the Forest Service sets and enforces its own National Forest management standards. Held closely accountable to no one, it has fallen prey to powerful timber interests and its own professional bias. Its resulting emphasis on timber production has antagonized millions of Americans.

In response to criticism, the Forest Service has embarked on an ambitious planning effort to guarantee better protection of nontimber forest values. Whether or not this move will quiet the public uproar depends on the Service's willingness to include the public formally in the renovation of its management goals and programs. Thus far, convinced that professionals alone should manage the National Forests, it has refrained from doing so.

APPALACHIA LOSES AGAIN *

The Forest Service's abrasive dealings with the residents of Appalachia illustrate its reluctance to advance from public relations to public involvement. The Weeks Act of 1911 authorizes the Forest Service to purchase forested, cutover, or denuded lands within the watersheds of navigable streams for the "regulation of the flow of navigable streams or for the production of timber." [18] In the pursuance of this Act, the Forest Service has acquired more than 5,155,000 acres in the Appalachian Mountains of Georgia, Kentucky, Tennessee, South and North Carolina, Virginia, and West Virginia.[19] Agency planners view the eight National Forests comprising these lands as an "Appalachian Greenbelt" serving the populous eastern seaboard:

> The concept of the Appalachian Greenbelt is possible because of the unique physiographic characteristics of the area. It is a mountainous green oasis in the Eastern United States from which flows a continuous supply of renewable resources and which provides the large surrounding population with a place to recreate in a natural setting. . . . Summer mountain temperatures are generally 10° lower than the adjacent plains. This factor makes the mountains a highly desirable retreat for city dwellers and other nearby residents.[20]

The Greenbelt acquisition policy, which from a national standpoint might seem farsighted, ignores the urgent needs of the ten million Americans who live in Appalachia. The policy assumes that the geography of the region cannot sustain economic development:

* This section is based on material provided by Si Kahn, a community development consultant in Mineral Bluff, Georgia.

> Population losses within the Greenbelt can be attrib-
> uted to the fact that this area can only sustain a
> limited number of people year-round. Many of the
> narrow mountain valleys are unsuitable for indus-
> trial complexes. Plans for economic development must
> recognize the limitations of the area so that over-
> emphasis on the wrong type of activities does not
> occur.[21]

One Appalachian reformer vehemently disputes the Forest
Service's assessment:

> To write off industrial development for the Southern
> Mountains because of their "narrow mountain valleys"
> is like saying that Pittsburgh can't support industry
> because of its many residential neighborhoods. In fact,
> Appalachia is for many reasons—raw material, elec-
> tric power, access to population centers, transporta-
> tion, labor force—ideally suited for tremendous in-
> dustrial growth. By ignoring the facts, the Forest
> Service is actively undermining the efforts of the ten
> million people who live in the mountains at economic,
> political, and social self-development.[22]

What makes the land acquisition policy intolerable to
Appalachian residents is that they, not the city-dwellers
who benefit from the policy, are called upon to pay for it.
Every time the Forest Service purchases land, it wipes out
a portion of the local tax base, and increases the tax burden
of local property owners. In the fifty Appalachian counties
containing at least forty thousand acres of National Forest
land, shrinking tax revenues have prevented improvement
of substandard public services. Soaring tax rates have
forced many property owners to sell, often to the Forest
Service, thus completing the vicious cycle. Thus the Forest
Service contributes to the region's economic stagnation and
to the migration of its sons and daughters, in search of
jobs, to the cities.

The Forest Service does make periodic payments, in lieu
of taxes, to these counties where National Forest timber is
harvested; 25 percent of the annual receipts of timber
sales are returned for construction of schools and roads.
Counties in the western United States, where timber cutting is heavy, sometimes get more from the Forest Service
rebates than they ever would from taxes. But since the

National Forests in the East produce far less timber and of poorer quality, Appalachian counties obtain from the Forest Service a mere fraction of potential tax revenues. In 1971, for example, the Forest Service paid Polk County, Tennessee, $32,740—22¢ per acre—for timber cutting in Cherokee National Forest, which covers more than half the county. Private landowners, in contrast, paid taxes totaling $1,500,000—$11.76 per acre—on considerably less land.[23]

Other federal programs involving land acquisition generously reimburse local governments for reductions in their property tax base. The Tennessee Valley Authority, for instance, makes payments to the states in which it acquires land which, by statute:

> shall not be less than the higher of (1) the average of state, county, municipal and district property taxes levied by them on purchased property and on the portion of TVA reservoir land allocated to power for the last two years such property was in private ownership or (2) $10,000.[24]

Consequently, for lands covering one-eightieth the area of National Forest lands in the county, the TVA paid Polk County, Tennessee, $225,766—almost seven times the Forest Service payment.[25] Similarly, under the "impacted areas" program, the federal government makes payments to school districts containing military bases and other large government installations in lieu of taxes. Its measure of payments, like the TVA's, approximates potential tax revenues: "Maximum entitlement is the product of the applicant's current expense tax rate applied to the estimated assessed valuation of the Federal property (exclusive of improvements since transfer date)." In FY 1970, the last year for which figures are available, 4,508 school districts scattered across the country picked up $587.2 million in aid from this program.[26]

The tying of Forest Service tax replacements to the level of timber production not only provides Appalachian communities with less compensation than either potential tax revenues or the TVA and impacted areas payments. It also gives the Forest Service a political incentive to boost timber cutting in the eastern National Forests—a move which both urban recreationists and Appalachian leaders oppose.

Other Forest Service practices in the Appalachian Mountains conflict with local needs. One is the charging of fees, ranging from one dollar a day to ten dollars a year, for use of National Forest recreational areas. As a result, most poor mountain families cannot afford to use the forest recreational facilities built in their own counties. Commenting on a Forest Service plan to build campsites in his area, one northern Georgia man warned: "There's a lot of old mountain people besides me who aren't going to take kindly to the idea of getting a permit to go on to land they call home." [27]

Appalachian working people also criticize the Forest Service's method of auctioning National Forest timber. By requiring bidders to post a large "bid bond," the Forest Service discriminates against the small logging operators who cannot afford to lay aside such amounts. The requirement that the winner in the bidding post a "performance bond"—sometimes equaling the full purchase price—often prevents all but the largest timber companies from bidding on the contract in the first place.

Forest Service practices in Appalachia add to the misery of a people long exploited by timber and mining interests and forgotten by the rest of America. Partly because a diminished private land base has stunted economic growth, the Appalachian counties containing National Forest land are among the country's poorest. The fourteen Appalachian counties with over 40 percent National Forest land support average populations of about nine thousand. Their average rate of poverty, according to the 1970 census, is 29.2 percent—more than twice the national average. [28]

Appalachian working people have not accepted their lot passively. Local newspapers, government officials, and poverty workers have repeatedly called on the Forest Service to pay more attention to local needs. One recent conflict over the acquisition of forest land led a Forest Service official to bulldoze and bury the trailer home of Vernon McCall, a disabled resident of Balsam Grove, North Carolina. According to a May 1971 story in the Atlanta *Constitution*:

> The Forest Service claimed the government owned the land, not Vernon, and they had been trying to get him off it since 1968. But the community lawyer said

no legal action has been taken to evict Vernon, and local authorities proceeded to charge Forest Ranger Dan W. Hile with willful injury to personal property.

Meantime Vernon, who is 40, has rented a new trailer, and scratches out a living on welfare and what he can make picking and selling ivy. And the seedlings the Forest Service planted over his old trailer have died.[29]

The Commissioner of Roads and Revenues of Fannin County, Georgia—which receives 24.2¢ per acre for the 42 percent of its land held in National Forests—has summed up local feelings about Forest Service land acquisition:

> They purchase private land as it becomes available with our Federal tax money, and use it in fact to undermine the local tax sources where our local revenue must come from to support our local government. . . .
>
> We can no longer ignore the seriousness of these problems. There must be some compatible adjustments when land is acquired and results in a revenue loss.[30]

Responding editorially to the Commissioner's remarks, an Appalachian newspaper, the *Blue Ridge Summit-Post,* wrote:

> Federal preservation of forest land is a good thing; we believe in some land control; but taxes are taxes, and Fannin County is having to strain the wrong pay check. Our residents work hard for their living, and carrying the load for the Forest Service is not helping the situation.[31]

The county judge of Polk County, Tennessee, was even more blunt in criticizing the Forest Service for perpetuating Appalachia's dearth of public services and jobs:

> In my opinion, I think the U.S. Government through the U.S. Forest Service, has helped in creating the underdeveloped or poverty areas by their system of buying and holding land within the Appalachian region.[32]

Traditionally, the Forest Service implemented National Forest management plans in Appalachia without consulting the local government or citizenry. Lately, in response to public pressure, it has begun holding "listening sessions" at which local residents are asked to present their views. But the Forest Service selects as a final plan one of several proposals it has drawn up *before* inviting public comment on all the proposals. Moreover, the agency's frequent failure to make printed transcripts of the listening sessions suggests that the public views there expressed receive only fleeting, on-the-spot consideration in the planning process. After attending a recent session, one north Georgia county official angrily wrote the Forest Service: "The Forest Service [has] never attempted to work with local government on future plans for U.S. Forest Service lands within their political subdivision." [33]

FOREST PLANNERS AND THE PUBLIC

The Forest Service's answer to criticism that it does no more than inform the public has been to promulgate new management guidelines for public involvement. In a February 1972 brochure entitled *Inform and Involve*, the Washington Office urges field officials to:

> Establish a procedure that will facilitate early identification of activities and issues that are of potential current interest;
> Broaden communication with TV, Radio, and press contacts;
> Seek out opportunities for Forest Service officials to speak out on current issues, correct erroneous information, and explain programs;
> Broaden contacts, with groups, associations, and organizations to better Inform and Involve a wide range of the public on current programs, projects, and issues. [34]

An accompanying *Guide to Public Involvement in Decision Making* suggests to field officials a number of ways to include the public in management decisions. [35] These include formal public hearings (printed transcript kept), public meetings, small invitational meetings, advisory committees, "advice-seeking visits with keymen," "letter request for comments," "utilizing the forum provided by other organizations," and "use of non-Forest Service groups to conduct studies of Forest Service programs and on-the-ground activities."

The *Guide* emphasizes that the choice of involvement method is entirely up to the local Forest Service official. It notes that statutes require formal hearings in wilderness area reviews and the preparation of environmental impact statements. In connection with other management actions, the *Guide* virtually prohibits the holding of formal public hearings—probably the most effective means of obtaining a broad cross-section of public views:

> Since the [hearing] record is costly to produce, tends to slow down the decision-making process, and provides information that can be obtained through less complicated and less costly methods, the formal hearing will not be used except where required by Congressional directives or where the decision-making level is higher than the region.

Another shortcoming of the *Guide* is its failure to specify which types of management decisions—other than the ones mentioned by statute—require the Forest Service official to solicit public comment. The *Guide* does suggest the holding of listening sessions in the "early stage" of multiple-use plan preparation and for the printing of "a synopsis of oral testimony." But what about specific actions taken in pursuance of a plan—such as timber sales, approvals of clearcutting, watershed treatments, construction of recreation facilities, approval of mining and grazing permits, road building, and the setting aside of new wilderness areas? The *Guide* does not reveal which, if any, of these actions require public involvement in their planning. It is reasonable to suppose from the *Guide*'s emphasis on avoiding *costly* public involvement efforts that field managers may minimize or omit such efforts in the case of specific management actions. As the previous discussions of the clearcutting and wilderness controversies indicate, public acceptance of National Forest management turns on the quality of these small-scale actions.

Despite its somewhat vague and fully voluntary message, the *Guide* does reflect the Forest Service's new determination to open up its decision process at least a crack. Under a section headed, "Attitudes Conducive to Successful Public Involvement," the *Guide* urges field officials to:

> Recognize that public involvement is an essential part of decision making since it enables the decision maker to render a better decision.
>
> Discard any notion that action which will affect environmental quality or the public interest can be judged only by professionals. Though a proposed action may be professionally correct, public concern may well outweigh professional considerations and justify proposal modification.
>
> Recognize that public involvement requires that it must be sought out *before* a decision has been reached.

These suggestions contrast sharply with Monongahela National Forest supervisor Frederick Dorrell's insistence, in the face of near unanimous public and Congressional censure, that professional good judgment demanded the continuance of clearcutting. Nevertheless, the *Guide*'s caveat to its enumeration of "conducive attitudes" illustrates the weakness of the entire "inform and involve" program—its failure to guarantee a clear public role in the making of *final* decisions:

> Do not feel that you, as a Forest Service officer, are in any way abdicating responsibilities in making management decisions because you have involved the public as a factor in reaching these decisions. The final decision is still up to you.

Not all professional foresters subscribe to the Forest Service's conception of the professional as policy-maker. Arnold W. Bolle, professor and former dean of the University of Montana School of Forestry, told the Senate Subcommittee on Forests in June 1972:

> In my opinion, the professional in any field—education, health, defense, or forestry and natural resources—has an important but specific role to play. He carries out the demands of society in his area of expertise, he lets the public know the opportunities and possibilities available for choice in setting policies and he can inform and warn the public of the consequences of the choices it may make. But he is no better qualified than the general public in deciding what is good for the public or what it ought to do (within safe limits) with the forests and related resources of forest lands. In making such decisions the public should and needs to be involved.[36]

The call for greater public participation in forest management decisions reflects the widening gap between the public's and the Forest Service's perceptions of the agency's vague multiple-use mandate. Fierce controversies over clearcutting and wilderness preservation might never have arisen, if Congress had legislated strict policy standards to govern the Forest Service. Instead, it granted the agency sweeping powers of legislation and policy-making. As Yale Law School Professor Charles A. Reich, observed ten years ago:

> The standards Congress has used to delegate authority over the forests are so general, so sweeping, and so vague as to represent a turnover of virtually all responsibility. "Multiple use" does establish that the forests cannot be used exclusively for one purpose, but beyond this it is little more than a phrase expressing the hope that all competing interests can somehow be satisfied and leaving the real decisions to others. The "relative values" of various resources are to be given "due consideration," but Congress has not indicated what those values are or what action shall be deemed "due consideration." Congress has directed "harmonious and coordinated management of the various resources," but it has left the Forest Service to deal with the problem that different uses of resources often clash rather than harmonize. Most significantly, Congress has told the Forest Service to "best meet the needs of the American people," but has left it entirely up to the Service to determine what those needs are.[37]

Not surprisingly, the Forest Service, like many groups of professionals in government, has used its broad authority to lean heavily toward one of the various conflicting elements of the public it serves—the timber industry. Its officials' natural tendency to view forest issues from a forester's perspective—which for many years has meant thinking in terms of productivity—has made them less receptive to the views of the lay public. Finally, as Reich points out, Forest Service officials, like other professional managers, are inclined to think of themselves as owners: "It is an easy step from here to the feeling that they alone know what is best."

In responding to charges of high-handedness and bias,

Forest Service officials have long pointed to their adherence to carefully prepared multiple-use management plans. The *Forest Service Manual* used to require every forest ranger to draft periodic management plans reflecting the capacity of his district's land to support resource uses in varying combinations and intensities.[38] Theoretically, the multiple-use plan would govern the execution of specific projects—such as timber sales, watershed treatments, and construction of recreational facilities.

In fact, these plans have rarely done more than bestow a multiple-use blessing on timber management activities ordained all along. The separately formulated "timber management plans" have controlled the quantity and quality of logging in the national forests, not the multiple-use plans. At the height of the Monongahela National Forest clear-cutting controversy, a Forest Service review team discovered that "the areas publicly criticized were cut *before* multiple use plans were prepared." [39] The limited design of the multiple-use plan guarantees its failure as an instrument of management coordination. Drafted by a forest ranger to cover only his district over a five-year period, the multiple-use plan does not stand a chance of governing the timber-management plan, which is drafted by the higher-ranking forest supervisor to cover a multidistrict working circle over a ten-year period.

Faulted increasingly for its timber production bias, the Forest Service began several years ago to acknowledge the shortcomings of its dual planning process. An agency task force concluded in October 1971, "If any overall criticism of past practice is in order, it is that the effort going into the development of coordinated plans for the management of the National Forests has been inadequate." [40] That same year, the agency's Wyoming Forest Study Team reported:

> Too frequently we found that management objectives were not clearly understood or defined. The decision to build a new road into a previously unroaded drainage, for example, was likely to be based on the use and protection of timber, without adequate consideration of other values. Opportunities were sought to "get the land under management," but action was often started before the Forest or District staff had defined what they were going to manage for.[41]

Likewise, the Bitterroot National Forest task force found that the forest's "multiple use planning is not far enough advanced." [42]

On November 9, 1971, the Chief of the Forest Service dispatched to the regional foresters an "emergency directive," instituting a new multiple-use planning process.[43] The new process stresses management coordination from the establishment of Servicewide objectives to the supervision of minor logging projects. It begins at the level of the "planning unit," a portion of a National Forest defined by one or more stream drainages. A multidisciplinary team —including a soil scientist, a wildlife biologist, a silviculturist, a recreation specialist, and others—surveys each unit. It maps the area by its soil, water, vegetation, and wildlife habitat types, and evaluates its productive capabilities, its current resources, and the public needs associated with it. Using this information and following the general policy directives of the regional forester and the more detailed "coordinating requirements" of the forest supervisor, the team formulates at least three alternative management plans: no development, partial development, and maximum development. Its report must "analyze the differences among alternative plans to show tradeoffs among the various planning objectives."

The responsible Forest Service "line officer"—in most cases, the forest ranger (several ranger districts make up each national forest)—then selects a management alternative on the basis of objectives and policy preferences provided by his superiors and the public. Next, the chosen unit plan is subjected to an "environmental analysis." The line officer files with the Council on Environmental Quality and announces in the *Federal Register* (the daily official journal of executive branch activities) the availability to the public of a draft environmental impact statement describing the plan and its anticipated effects on the natural environment. After considering any comments received from other agencies (notably, the Environmental Protection Agency, which is concerned about potential air and water pollution), groups, and individuals, the ranger files with the CEQ and releases to the public a final environmental impact statement. Upon the approval of the forest supervisor, the unit plan becomes part of that National Forest's new multiple-use plan.

The new planning process clearly improves upon the old dual system of multiple-use and timber-management plans. It replaces single-resource planning with planning by multidisciplinary teams. Upon completion, its computerized system for collecting and displaying ecological and sociological data will enable Forest Service officials to make planning decisions on the basis of more accurate and complete information. The new process also increases the participation of other natural resource agencies and private citizens in National Forest management. Perhaps most importantly, it clearly identifies the conflicts and trade-offs among alternative uses of the same lands and their varying impacts on the environment.

But the new process contains some flaws. The emergency directive places a premium on the "accuracy, scope, and balance" of planning data. Not surprisingly, since the National Forests cover one-tenth of the country's surface area, the gaps in existing data are many and wide. The Forest Service lacks reliable information on what the public wants and needs from the National Forests throughout the country, it possesses only imprecise sample data on the fifty-six million acres of undeveloped roadless areas in the National Forest System, and its own recent research indicates that there are major inaccuracies in its resource inventories of developed land. Nevertheless, feeling the bite of Presidential budget cutting, the Forest Service leadership, since issuance of the emergency directive, has ordered field planners to "use existing resource information except where new field inventories must be made to fill critical data gaps." Unit plans formulated under this policy cannot help but continue the imbalances among uses and environmental blunders of the past.

The Environmental Protection Agency and numerous conservationists have criticized the early unit plans for their lack of detail in describing upcoming developmental activities and their environmental impacts. The typical plan will say, "The management of this subunit will emphasize recreation and wildlife values with timber harvesting limited to that which will enhance the favored resource values," but will not describe the exact recreation, wildlife, or timber management projects contemplated. Without consideration of such projects, the unit plans' analyses of potential environmental impacts are necessarily imprecise as well.

Second, the Forest Service's designation of three "multi-objectives," developed by the Water Resources Council for federal water projects, as the fundamental goals of new multiple-use planning from unit to regional levels, is unwise and possibly illegal. These multiobjectives—"to enhance national economic development," "to enhance regional development," and "to enhance the quality of the environment"—bear scant resemblance to the objectives established for National Forest management by the Multiple Use–Sustained Yield Act. Since two out of three of the multiobjectives involve economic development, their use in multiple-use planning in place of the statutory purposes may prejudice management prescriptions in favor of commodity resource development (timber and range) and against noncommodity resource development (water, recreation, and wildlife). It is possible that use of the multiobjectives in unit planning thereby constitutes a violation of the Multiple Use Act.[44]

To prevent Forest Supervisors from evading or improperly revising their multiple-use plans, the new planning process calls for new policy-making criteria and greater public involvement. The regional foresters' planning area guides to the forest supervisors will include:

> *Basic Assumptions.* These are statements which recognize the future nature of society as relates to social, economic, and environmental factors, especially as will exist in relation to the Planning Area. They will provide a recognition of the conditions we expect in the future.
> *Coordinating Criteria.* This section of the guide contains statements of opportunities and constraints to be applied in carrying out the more intensive planning of the Planning Units.[45]

Considering its statutory role as a forest management agency, the Forest Service is hardly equipped to establish accurate and equitable "basic assumptions" about the "future nature of society." Trend evaluation, value-setting, and policy-making have traditionally been the prerogatives of elected officials—the President and the Congress. By usurping these functions, the Forest Service opens itself to crippling informal pressure from the timber industry and other powerful interest groups.

The new process invites, but does not guarantee, formal public participation in plan formulation.[46] The emergency directive refers the officials to the Forest Service's *Guide to Public Involvement,* which merely suggests the holding of public listening sessions. The public will have no defined right to participate in the all-important planning at any stage. Its ability to propose alternative plans and to influence both the choice of a final plan and the review of that choice will depend solely upon the patience and open-mindedness of the hundreds of agency officials involved.

The old planning process never attempted to subordinate timber production to the overall effort to match forest resources with public needs. It merely followed in the wake of the loggers, apologizing for their environmental destruction, and proposing cosmetic measures to conceal it. The *new* process provides machinery which, if somewhat revised, could for the first time ensure real control and coordination of *all* forest activities. Unfortunately, this machinery thrives on the pure dollars-and-cents considerations of timber management. It could just as easily, perhaps inadvertently, maintain the supremacy of timber production in National Forest management. Throughout the planning process—from the designation of "basic assumptions" and "coordinating criteria" to the reviewing of final plan decisions—the Forest Service will have to weigh commodity uses against noncommodity uses. The inescapable fact that the value of wilderness, recreation, and other noncommodity uses cannot be quantified will make an objective weighing impossible. Charges of favoritism toward the commodity uses will continue. Urgently needed is a value estimator suited to both commodity and noncommodity uses, enabling the Forest Service to grant equal consideration to each of the five major National Forest uses.

Barring the unlikely invention of such a measure, Congress may have to assume the burden of deciding what mix of uses in what areas best serves the public interest. It could do so by establishing a general ranking of uses to be applied in all management decisions, by directing the Forest Service to manage for a single dominant use a specified number of acres meeting specified natural criteria and distributed geographically in a specified pattern, or by directing the Forest Service to submit to Congress for review alternative long-range management plans for each National Forest or other unit formulated under an assumption of equal consideration of all uses.

The last mentioned might prove the best avenue to a National Forest management scheme which genuinely serves the interests of all Americans. It would permit the public to participate fully in the adoption of management plans and hold the Forest Service accountable for its actions in specific forest areas. Congressional review and authorization of specific agency project proposals is common in the fields of defense and irrigation–water power. Since 1964, Congress has also acted individually upon Forest Service recommendations for new wilderness areas.

In many of these cases, of course, Congressional review has been cursory, with the sponsoring agency's justification for its project accepted on its face. To ensure that the proposed National Forest management plans presented to Congress adequately reflect public sentiment, Congress may have to legislate procedures for substantive public involvement in the early stages of Forest Service planning. These might include mandatory public hearings with transcripts printed and distributed, formal opportunities for citizens and interested federal and state agencies to have their independent proposals considered and reviewed by the Forest Service, and formal opportunities for citizens and agencies to express their views during the various planning reviews conducted subsequent to public hearings.

Procedural reforms in National Forest management planning could leave unchanged the present inequality of timber and nontimber uses. Both the Forest Service and Congress could choose to ignore the advice of the public while going through the motions of listening. On the other hand, the reforms might so complicate and delay decision-making as to bring forest management to a standstill. Nevertheless, as Professor Reich has observed, "Bringing decisions out into the open is perhaps the greatest single insurance against arbitrariness. Secret decisions are not only undemocratic, they are also often unsound, for the agency, cut off from other points of view, may become the prisoner of its own preconceptions." [47]

6

🌲🌲

The Greening of the
Forest Service

In other words, our organization and our methods must never be frozen, but always subject to change. . . . Never change for the sake of change, but change for the sake of betterment the moment we were sure that betterment would follow change. The old battle cry of bureaucracy, "We have always done it this way," meant nothing to the men of the Forest Service.[1]

> Gifford Pinchot, first Chief of
> the Forest Service, 1947

The August 1972 release of a new long-range management plan for Montana's embattled Bitterroot National Forest took conservationists by surprise. They had been expecting a renewed defense of clearcutting and accelerated timber harvests, but, in tone at least (details of the plan will be revealed over the next several years in twenty-eight watershed "unit plans"), Forest Supervisor Orville L. Daniels surrendered his ax:

> We should manage the National Forests with a respect for the land, knowing man to be a part of the natural process, not a master of ecological systems. . . . Only after the fullest possible understanding and an evaluation of gains and losses, should any change in the ecosystem be made. . . .
>
> It is clear in analyzing what we have been told by the public that recognition of intangible amenity values such as scenic beauty, solitude, the absence of air, water, and noise pollution is an integral part of ethical land management. The perception to recognize and provide for enhancement and protection of these intangible values must be developed as part of our land ethic.
>
> It is clear that production of commodities is an in-

132

tegral part of quality land management and that the
land ethic should provide for these economic considerations. In doing so, it is important that we base our
management in accordance with the capability of the
land rather than for short term resource needs. . . .
Whenever possible, we should preserve management
options for future generations.[2]

Talk of the need for a "land ethic"—talk which, several
years ago, Forest Service officials would have labeled "ex-
tremist" or "preservationist"—today is standard lingo in the
Service's campaign to regain the public's trust. The new
concern for environmental quality and public involvement
in National Forest management arrived with former Chief
Cliff's remarkable admission in September 1970 that "our
programs are out of balance to meet public needs for the
environmental 1970's and we are receiving mounting criticism from all sides. Our direction must be and is being
changed." [3]

Shortly thereafter, the Forest Service launched a new
multiple-use planning project to chart the long-range protection and development of the National Forests, watershed
by watershed, with close reference to the capability of the
land and the express desires of the public. Recently, the
Forest Service rescinded a proposal, formulated with little
consideration of negative impacts on nontimber forest uses,
to boost National Forest timber cutting by one-half over the
next ten years. Although the agency continues to promote
accelerated timber production it has pledged to increase
allowable cut only as intensive forest practices, designed
to spur tree growth, are actually implemented. In response
to public complaints about clearcutting, the agency announced an "action plan" to ensure the protection of environmental and nontimber values in timber harvesting and
road construction. It also revamped its regulations to require timber purchasers to utilize fully the trees chopped
down and to preserve the soil, water, trees, and scenery left
behind. It began researching aerial logging methods to be
applied where the construction of roads would cause intolerable erosion. The Forest Service at last surveyed the many
roadless areas in the National Forests and set aside 235
of them for further study leading to possible designation as
Wilderness Areas. In both multiple-use planning and the

identification of New Wilderness Study Areas, the Forest
Service reached out for public comment as it never had
before.

Forward-thinking Chief John R. McGuire and his associates might well have achieved further reform, were it not
for the forces which have always impeded balanced management of the National Forests. For the fifth straight year,
President Nixon severely reduced the Forest Service's
urgent request for funds, and Congress reluctantly acqui-
esced. The timber industry, sniffing a windfall in the timber
price rise caused by a home-building boom, redoubled its
lobbying in Washington, D.C., and at the local level for
increased National Forest timber cutting. And due to the
paucity and vagueness of the statutes and regulations
governing National Forest management, field officials remained vulnerable to industry pressure. Some officials, to
the dismay of Forest Service leaders and the public, took
advantage of their broad authority to set their own management priorities and to exclude the public from policy-
making.

To inject into National Forest management a greater
sensitivity for the environmental quality and the public's
express desires, Congress and the Forest Service should
take the following actions:

Provide Congressional guidance
to the Forest Service.

1. Congress, perhaps through a special joint committee of legislators knowledgeable about interior,
agriculture, and environmental affairs, should thoroughly examine National Forest management policies.
After considering evidence gathered through reports
from the Forest Service, the Environmental Protection
Agency, the Interior Department, and other relevant
federal and state agencies, and through public hearings held in Washington, D.C., and around the country, the committee should draft a new Forest Service
organic act, establishing goals and providing management direction (particularly, clear procedures for
land use planning, consideration of environmental
impacts, and public initiation and review of management proposals) with greater precision than the Multiple Use–Sustained Yield Act of 1960.

2. Congress should consider establishing a Department of Conservation, embracing the Forest Service, the National Park Service, the Bureau of Sport Fisheries and Wildlife, and the Bureau of Outdoor Recreation, and dedicated to protecting the environment and conserving natural resources for limited use—especially wilderness and recreation.

Supply the Forest Service with
more generous, balanced funding.

3. To make possible genuine multiple-use management, including nearly all the suggested reforms that follow, the President and Congress must fund the Forest Service at a much higher level and with far greater balance among management activities than at present. The Forest Service, in turn, must calculate better the level of funding needed for quality multiple-use management, and must lobby aggressively with the President and Congress to obtain it. If the Forest Service eventually receives less money than it requires to do a good job, it should reduce the quantity, not the quality, of its accomplishments proportionately.

Diminish the likelihood of management errors
by increasing the accountability of
Forest Service officials to the agency leadership,
Congress, and the public.

4. Operating under basic assumptions about society's future needs and broad policy constraints, and through procedures guaranteeing both full consideration of management proposals other than the one initially selected and broad public participation in the formulation and selection of alternative plans—all of which Congress should specify through legislation—the Forest Service should accelerate its preparation of multiple-use management plans for every National Forest watershed. As each National Forest completes its multiple-use plan (the composite of the forest's many watershed unit plans), the Forest Service should forward it to Congress for approval before acting on any of its provisions.

5. Congress should specify procedures for periodic

review and modification of Forest Service plans, including full public participation.

6. The Forest Service should increase the frequency and depth of field inspections and should regularly commission teams of private foresters, soil and water scientists, wildlife biologists, recreation specialists, and social scientists to review and criticize its performance in various activities and geographical areas. The agency should strongly discipline field officials who violate management plans, statutes, or regulations, and reward those officials who follow the book imaginatively but closely.

7. Congress should require of the Forest Service an annual report discussing the previous year's accomplishments and the agency's proposed actions for the short and long term. This report should be distinct from and more detailed than the "justification statement" filed each year with the House and Senate Appropriations Committees.

Intensify formal public involvement in National Forest management.

8. Congress should create a National Forest Advisory Council, which, through public hearings held throughout the country each year, correspondence with interested citizens and groups, and investigations of controversial Forest Service actions, would funnel public comment on National Forest management to the Chief of the Forest Service, Congress, and the President. The part-time Council, which should be provided an ample, full-time staff, might include four private citizens appointed for a set term by the Speaker of the House of Representatives and three appointed by the President, with as many National Forest user groups as possible represented.

9. As already suggested, Congress and the Forest Service together should establish procedures for extensive public involvement in National Forest planning and decision-making, including full access to preparatory memoranda as well as final documents, the right to initiate planning and management proposals, and the right to comment on the review of draft and final proposals.

10. The Forest Service itself should be required by Congress to hold formal public hearings—with transcripts kept for public examination and copying—at least once a year in each National Forest and in Washington, D.C., to solicit comment on its management activities.

11. The Forest Service should appoint a Deputy Chief in Washington, an assistant regional forester in each region, and an assistant forest supervisor in each National Forest to act as ombudsmen. Their sole duties— *not* to include public information and education— would be to gather public comment on Forest Service activities, listen to complaints, relay them directly to the Chief, regional forester, or forest supervisor, and seek action on them whenever possible.

Reduce Forest Service officials' vulnerability to informal political pressuring.

12. In addition to the actions already recommended, Congress should abolish the practice of returning 25 percent of timber sale receipts to the counties in which timber is cut. It should replace these payments with more equitable and dependable federal grants— the size to be determined by the number of county residents, the local property tax rate, and the amount of otherwise taxable land belonging to the National Forest—to *all* counties embracing National Forest land, regardless of the amount of timber cutting.

13. The Forest Service should require its officials to keep detailed records of their personal contacts with all non-Service persons and to make the records available for public inspection.

Further protect and enhance the National Forest environment.

14. The Forest Service should postpone expansion of the nationwide annual allowable cut until new multiple-use plans are completed for every National Forest. The agency should file an environmental impact statement with the Council on Environmental Quality and obtain the specific approval of Congress for every proposed increase in the nationwide allowable cut.

15. Inviting testimony by the Forest Service, private

foresters, and other interested parties, Congress should investigate Forest Service procedures for classifying commercial timberland and regulating timber harvesting (including allowable cut formulation) and amend them so as to eliminate the potential for political or economic bias in sustained yield calculations.

16. Until a new multiple-use plan is adopted for a particular National Forest unit, the Forest Service should file an environmental impact statement for every timber sale valued at more than $100,000 or threatening severe injury to the environment or non-timber uses, and should prepare an in-Service environmental analysis report for every smaller sale within that unit.

17. The Forest Service should minimize its use of clearcutting—particularly east of the Great Plains where recreation use abounds—and banish it from areas of outstanding scenic beauty, areas subject to severe erosion, areas with critical wildlife habitat or projected intensive recreational use, and areas where regeneration will be difficult or impossible.

18. Where clearcutting is practiced, the clearcuts should be kept to a size that will minimize harm to the forest soil, water, vegetation, wildlife, and scenery, and except for emergency control of fire, insect, and disease attacks, they should not exceed twenty-five acres.

19. The Forest Service, with the financial assistance of Congress, should accelerate its research into the environmental impacts of clearcutting and the feasibility of replacing much of it with shelterwood and group selection cutting. The agency should also speed up its development of aerial logging systems to reduce the mileage of logging roads constructed in the National Forests.

20. The Forest Service should employ more specialists —geologists, hydrologists, ecologists, recreation specialists, and landscape architects—in planning and supervising timber sales, road construction, and other major developmental projects.

21. In formulating watershed unit plans, the Forest Service should consider setting aside roadless areas for later study and possible designation as Wilderness

Areas in addition to the 235 New Wilderness Study Areas already protected from development.

22. The Forest Service should quickly identify, and Congress designate, additional Wilderness Areas in the National Forests east of the Great Plains.

23. The Forest Service should recommend to Congress for statutory protection large areas in the National Forests which could be withdrawn from timber production and managed for recreation use less restrictive than wilderness.

Stimulate production of wood
outside the National Forests.

24. The Forest Service should thoroughly investigate the costs and benefits, in dollars and timber volume, of (1) federal purchase and intensive management of some productive nonindustry private forest lands and (2) federal subsidization of private forest land management, in seeking an enlarged timber yield from nonindustry private lands. It should report its findings to Congress with detailed programs drawn up for both options.

25. Upon receipt of the Forest Service study, Congress should hold hearings and, assuming that a reasonable benefit-cost ratio is found, authorize and fund a purchase-and-management program, a subsidy program, or a program combining the two.

26. Congress should recognize in statutory form the need to protect all forest land—private as well as public—from logging practices abusive of aesthetic and environmental values. The statute should establish strict standards for harvesting timber, constructing logging roads, and restoring the land to its former condition (including mandatory reforestation), and empower the Environmental Protection Agency to inspect and enforce the standards. The statute should require owners of five thousand acres or more who are contemplating timber cutting to formulate plans describing the actions they will take to comply with the standards. Before proceeding with cutting operations, they should be required to submit the plans to the EPA for approval.

27. The Forest Service should expand its research into

ways of stretching the country's wood supply through greater recycling of wood products, fuller utilization of trees now being harvested, and the development of economically competitive substitutes for wood in home construction.

28. If wood product prices rise as a result of the changes in Forest Service policies here recommended, Congress should not respond by increasing the timber output of the National Forests. Such an action would only increase the inequities of an already unjust wood subsidy program. The current policy of managing marginally productive National Forest sites for timber production in effect subsidizes the loggers and wood processors involved as well as all wood users, whether or not they need assistance, by keeping the price of wood lower than it would be under free market conditions. If Congress deems a wood subsidy to be in the national interest, it should subsidize individual wood purchasers (such as home buyers) who actually need help, not all wood purchasers, as it does now. Moreover, such subsidies should come from general revenues, not in the form of long-term damage to the National Forest environment through excessive timber cutting.

These recommendations, once put into practice, would be the start of a new life for the National Forests. But the roar of the bulldozer will never yield to the burble of the mountain brook until Congress, the President, and the Forest Service banish from National Forest management its prologging bias and restore to it a genuine respect for the land. Confronted with persistent industry demands for more cutting, these political institutions cannot be expected to save the people's forests without the people's guidance and support. The vigilant citizens whose protestations jolted the Forest Service into self-examination and change now face a much harder task. They must persuade millions of their fellow public-forest owners to take an active interest for the first time in the protection of *their* National Forests —to applaud the management reforms already instituted and to push relentlessly for the many improvements still urgently needed.

Appendices

APPENDIX 1-1
U.S. Timber Inventories, Removals, and Growth (1970)

Growing Stock *

Type of Ownership	Softwood (Billion Cubic Feet)			Hardwood (Billion Cubic Feet)			Total (Billion Cubic Feet)		
	Inventory	Removals	Growth	Inventory	Removals	Growth	Inventory	Removals	Growth
National Forest	200	2.1	2.0	18	0.1	0.6	217	2.2	2.6
Other Public	48	.7	1.0	20	.2	.8	68	.9	1.7
Private—Forest Industry	73	3.1	2.6	27	.6	.9	100	3.7	3.5
Private—Farm and Other Nonindustry	110	3.7	5.1	153	3.5	5.7	264	7.2	10.8
Total	432	9.6	10.7	217	4.4	7.9	649	14.0	18.6

Sawtimber†

Type of Ownership	Softwood (Billion Board Feet)			Hardwood (Billion Board Feet)			Total (Billion Board Feet)		
	Inventory	Removals	Growth	Inventory	Removals	Growth	Inventory	Removals	Growth
National Forest	982	12.7	8.6	40	0.4	1.3	1022	13.2	9.9
Other Public	223	4.2	4.0	40	.6	1.7	263	4.8	5.6
Private—Forest Industry	318	16.3	10.0	68	1.9	2.4	386	18.2	12.4
Private—Farm and Other Nonindustry	382	14.4	17.7	368	12.1	14.3	751	26.6	32.0
Total	1905	47.7	40.3	515	15.0	19.7	2421	62.8	59.9

* Growing stock signifies all trees at least five inches in diameter of good form and vigor.
† Sawtimber signifies trees of sufficient size (9 inches or more in diameter) and of suitable form and solidness to be processed into lumber and plywood.
Note: Data may not add to totals because of rounding.
Source: Div. of Forest Economics and Marketing Research, Forest Service, U.S. Dept. of Agriculture, Washington, D.C. July 1973.

APPENDIX 1-2
Commercial Forest Land Ownership (1970)

Type of Ownership	Total U.S. Area	Proportion	North	South	Rocky Mountains	Pacific Coast
	Thousand acres	Percent	Thousand acres	Thousand acres	Thousand acres	Thousand acres
Federal:						
National Forest	91,924	18	10,458	10,764	39,787	30,915
Bureau of Land Management	4,762	1	75	11	2,024	2,652
Bureau of Indian Affairs	5,888	1	815	220	2,809	2,044
Other Federal	4,534	1	963	3,282	78	211
Total Federal	107,109	21	12,311	14,277	44,699	35,822
State	21,423	4	13,076	2,321	2,198	3,828
County and municipal	7,589	2	6,525	681	71	312
Forest industry	67,341	14	17,563	35,325	2,234	12,219
Farm	131,135	26	51,017	65,137	8,379	6,602
Miscellaneous private	165,101	33	77,409	74,801	4,051	8,840
All ownerships	499,697	100	177,901	192,542	61,632	67,622

Source: U.S. Department of Agriculture, Forest Service, *The Outlook for Timber in the United States*, draft, 1972.

APPENDIX 1-3

Multiple Use–Sustained Yield Act of 1960 (16 U.S.C. 528-531)

Sec. 1. It is the policy of the Congress that the national forests are established and shall be administered for outdoor recreation, range, timber, watershed, and wildlife and fish purposes. The purposes of this Act are declared to be supplemental to, but not in derogation of, the purposes for which the national forests were established as set forth in the Act of June 4, 1897 (16 U.S.C. 475). Nothing herein shall be construed as affecting the jurisdiction or responsibilities of the several States with respect to wildlife and fish on the national forests. Nothing herein shall be construed so as to affect the use or administration of the mineral resources of national forest lands or to affect the use or administration of Federal lands not within the national forests.

Sec. 2. The Secretary of Agriculture is authorized and directed to develop and administer the renewable surface resources of the national forests for multiple use and sustained yield of the several products and services obtained therefrom. In the administration of the national forests due consideration shall be given to the relative values of the various resources in particular areas. The establishment and maintenance of areas of wilderness are consistent with the purposes and provisions of this Act.

Sec. 3. In the effectuation of this Act the Secretary of Agriculture is authorized to cooperate with interested State and local governmental agencies and others in the development and management of the national forests.

Sec. 4. As used in this Act, the following terms shall have the following meanings:

(a) "Multiple use" means the management of all the various renewable surface resources of the national forests so that they are utilized in the combination that will best meet the needs of the American people; making the most judicious use of the land for some or all of these resources or related services over areas large enough to provide sufficient latitude for periodic adjustments in use to conform to changing needs and conditions; that some land will be used for less than all of the resources; and harmonious and coordinated management of the various resources, each with the other, without impairment of the productivity of the land, with consideration being given to the relative values of the various resources, and not necessarily the combination of uses that will give the greatest dollar return or the greatest unit output.

(b) "Sustained yield of the several products and services" means the achievement and maintenance in perpetuity of a high-level annual or regular periodic output of the various renewable resources of the national forests without impairment of the productivity of the land.

APPENDIX 1-4
Policy Directive

Contained in a Letter from the Secretary of Agriculture
to the Chief of the Forest Service
upon that Agency's creation, February 1, 1905

In the administration of the forest reserves, it must be clearly
borne in mind that all land is to be devoted to its most productive use for the permanent good of the whole people and not for
the temporary benefit of individuals or companies. All the resources of forest reserves are for use, and this use must be
brought about in a thoroughly prompt and businesslike manner,
under such restrictions only as will insure the permanence of
these resources.

The vital importance of forest reserves to the great industries
of the western states will be largely increased in the near future
by the continued steady advance in settlement and development.
The permanence of the resources of the reserves is therefore
indispensable to continued prosperity, and the policy of this
Department for their protection and use will invariably be
guided by this fact, always bearing in mind that the conservative use of these resources in no way conflicts with their permanent value.

You will see to it that the water, wood, and forage of the reserves are conserved and wisely used for the benefit of the
home-builder first of all; upon whom depends the best permanent use of the lands and resources alike. The continued prosperity of the agricultural, lumbering, mining and live-stock
interests is directly dependent upon a permanent and accessible
supply of water, wood, and forage, as well as upon the present
and future use of these resources under businesslike regulations,
enforced with promptness, effectiveness, and common sense.

In the management of each reserve local questions will be
decided upon local grounds; the dominant industry will be considered first, but with as little restriction to minor industries as
may be possible; sudden changes in industrial conditions will
be avoided by gradual adjustment after due notice; and where
conflicting interests must be reconciled, the question will always
be decided from the standpoint of the greatest good of the
greatest number in the long run.

Source: U.S. Department of Agriculture, *The Principal Laws Relating to the Establishment and Administration of the National Forests
and to Other Forest Service Activities,* Agriculture Handbook No. 20
(July 1964), p. 67.

U.S. Department of Agriculture, Forest Service, Major Activities

U.S. DEPARTMENT OF AGRICULTURE
FOREST SERVICE

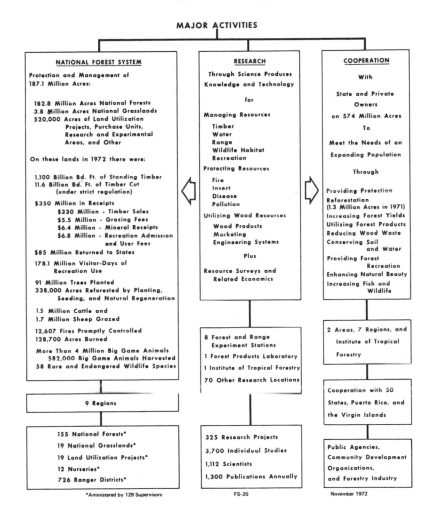

Source: Forest Service, "What the Forest Service Does," FS-20 (October 1970), p. 4.

APPENDIX 4-1
General Classification Key For Productive Forest Land

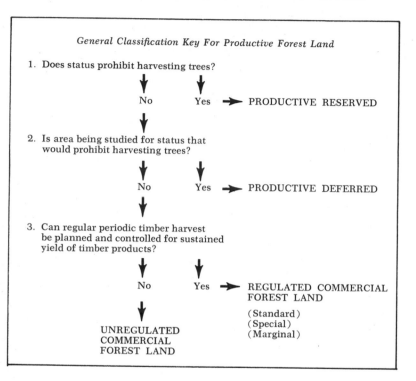

Source: Forest Service, *Forest Service Manual*, 1972.

APPENDIX 5-1

Forest Service Budget Estimates and Appropriations,
Fiscal Years 1955–1972

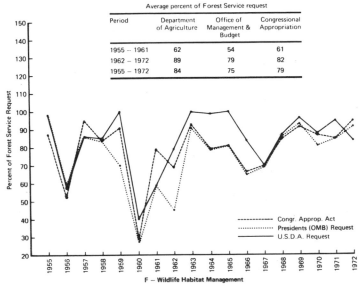

F — Wildlife Habitat Management

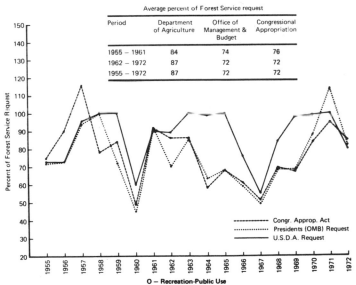

O — Recreation-Public Use

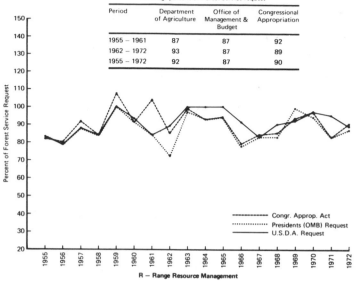

Average percent of Forest Service request

Period	Department of Agriculture	Office of Management & Budget	Congressional Appropriation
1955 – 1961	87	87	92
1962 – 1972	93	87	89
1955 – 1972	92	87	90

R – Range Resource Management

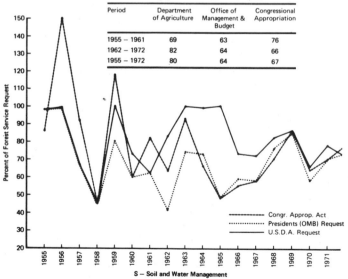

Average percent of Forest Service request

Period	Department of Agriculture	Office of Management & Budget	Congressional Appropriation
1955 – 1961	69	63	76
1962 – 1972	82	64	66
1955 – 1972	80	64	67

S – Soil and Water Management

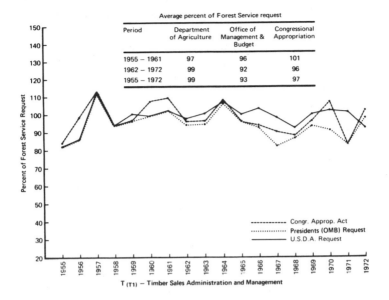

Average percent of Forest Service request

Period	Department of Agriculture	Office of Management & Budget	Congressional Appropriation
1955 – 1961	97	96	101
1962 – 1972	99	92	96
1955 – 1972	99	93	97

- - - - - Congr. Approp. Act
············ Presidents (OMB) Request
———— U.S.D.A. Request

T (T1) — Timber Sales Administration and Management

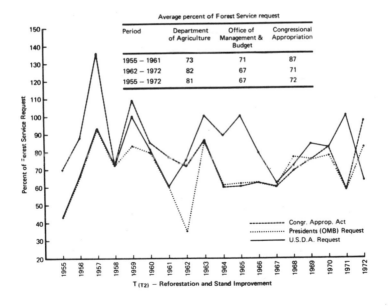

Average percent of Forest Service request

Period	Department of Agriculture	Office of Management & Budget	Congressional Appropriation
1955 – 1961	73	71	87
1962 – 1972	82	67	71
1955 – 1972	81	67	72

- - - - - Congr. Approp. Act
············ Presidents (OMB) Request
———— U.S.D.A. Request

T (T2) — Reforestation and Stand Improvement

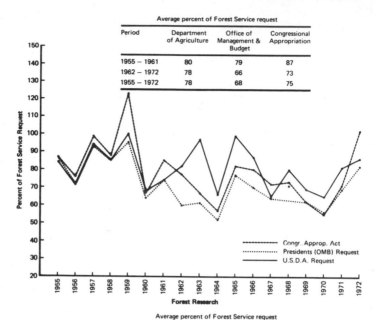

Forest Research

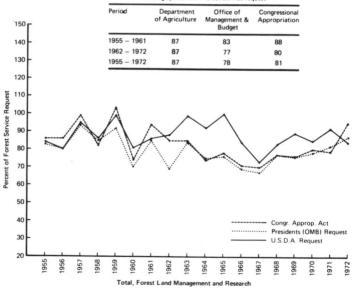

Total, Forest Land Management and Research

Source: Richard M. Alston, *FOREST—Goals and Decisionmaking in the Forest Service*, U.S. Department of Agriculture, Forest Service, Research Paper INT-128 (September, 1972), pp. 64–65.

Forest Service, USDA, and OMB Requests for FY 1974 Forest Service Budget
(in thousands)

Appropriation Item	FY 1973 Appropriation	FY 1974 Forest Service Request	FY 1974 Department of Agriculture Request	FY 1974 President's Budget (OMB Request)
FOREST PROTECTION AND UTILIZATION				
FOREST LAND MANAGEMENT:				
National Forest protection and management:				
Timber resource management:				
(a) Sales administration and management	$ 68,074	$ 77,545	$ 69,269	$ 69,469
(b) Reforestation and stand improvement	31,702	39,900	29,136	23,136
Recreation-public use	41,353	63,418	47,573	41,343
Wildlife habitat management	7,724	15,000	8,452	7,802
Rangeland management	14,561	16,700	14,787	14,287
Soil and water management	9,734	19,200	10,853	10,123
Mineral claims, leases, and special uses	5,657	10,600	8,017	6,667
Land classification, adjustments, and surveys	8,038	17,666	9,585	9,085
Forest fire protection	32,001	48,494	32,982	32,127
Maintenance of improvements for fire and general purposes (including communications)	7,795	11,800	9,100	8,576
Forest advanced logging and construction	5,000	9,600	—	—
Payments to Employees' Compensation Fund	2,131	2,300	2,300	2,300
Subtotal, National Forest protection and management	233,770	332,223	242,054	224,915
Water resource development related activities	4,022	6,800	4,022	4,022
Fighting forest fires	4,275	4,275	4,275	4,275
Insect and disease control	10,585	13,500	10,585	10,585
Cooperative law enforcement program	2,527	7,500	2,710	2,527
Total, Forest Land Management	255,179	364,298	263,646	246,324
FOREST RESEARCH:				
Forest and range management research:				
Timber management research	12,606	17,846	11,746	11,746
Watershed management research	6,616	8,497	6,266	6,266
Wildlife habitat and range research	4,588	6,773	3,473	3,473

APPENDIX 5-2 continued

Appropriation Item	FY 1973 Appropriation	FY 1974 Forest Service Request	FY 1974 Department of Agriculture Request	FY 1974 President's Budget (OMB Request)
Forest recreation research	1,353	3,203	1,103	1,103
Subtotal, Forest and range management research	25,163	36,319	22,588	22,588
Forest protection research:				
Fire and atmospheric sciences research	7,878	8,978	7,378	7,378
Forest insect and disease research	10,520	15,930	9,830	9,830
Subtotal, Forest protection research	18,398	24,908	17,208	17,208
Forest products and engineering research:				
Forest products utilization research	9,231	11,431	9,131	9,131
Forest engineering research	1,478	1,478	1,478	1,478
Subtotal, Forest products and engineering research	10,709	12,909	10,609	10,609
Forest resource economics research:				
Forest survey	3,433	5,033	3,433	3,433
Forest products marketing research	2,030	2,330	2,030	2,030
Forest economics research	1,407	3,407	1,407	1,407
Subtotal, Forest resource economics research	6,870	10,770	6,870	6,870
Total, Forest Research	61,140	84,906	57,275	57,275
STATE AND PRIVATE FORESTRY COOPERATION:				
Cooperation in forest fire control	25,000	30,000	24,000	16,000
Cooperation in forest tree planting	325	550	325	325
Cooperation in forest management and processing	5,000	10,000	5,000	5,000
General forestry assistance	2,435	5,660	2,435	2,435
Total State and Private Forestry Cooperation	32,760	46,210	31,760	23,760
TOTAL, FOREST PROTECTION AND UTILIZATION	349,079	495,414	352,681	327,359
COOPERATIVE RANGE IMPROVEMENTS	700	700	700	700
CONSTRUCTION AND LAND ACQUISITION:				
Development of recreation-public use areas:				
Budget authority	7,710	11,000	2,798	—
Program level	—	11,000	2,798	1,452.90
Water resource development construction:				
Budget authority	3,182	15,400	2,329	47

Program level	—	15,400	2,329	1,772
Construction for fire, administration, and other purposes:				
Budget authority	2,317	49,300	4,001	1,103
Program level	—	49,300	4,001	2,241
Research construction:				
Budget authority	5,143	16,091	394	—
Program level	—	16,091	394	134
Pollution abatement:				
Budget authority	29,470	31,300	31,300	23,148
Program level	—	31,300	31,300	31,300
Land acquisition, Weeks Act:				
Budget authority	1,300	1,380	1,300	1,200
Program level	—	1,380	1,300	1,200
TOTAL, CONSTRUCTION AND LAND ACQUISITION:				
Budget authority	48,582	124,471	42,122	25,498
Program level	—	124,471	42,122	38,099.9
FOREST ROADS AND TRAILS:				
Cash—Federal-Aid Highway Act	158,840	200,000	150,845	87,700
Program level	158,840	200,200	135,870	70,900
ACQUISITION OF LANDS FOR NATIONAL FOREST, SPECIAL ACTS	80	370	294	94
ACQUISITION OF LANDS TO COMPLETE LAND EXCHANGES	—	55	55	55
ASSISTANCE TO STATES FOR TREE PLANTING	1,020	2,500	1,020	1,020
CONSTRUCTION AND OPERATION OF RECREATION FACILITES	—	3,546	2,925	3,546
SCIENTIFIC ACTIVITIES OVERSEAS (special foreign currency program)	—	3,000	3,000	1,000
YOUTH CONSERVATION CORPS	3,500	30,000	—	10,000
ADDITIONAL PROGRAMS PROPOSED:				
Surface Environment and Mining	—	6,800	—	—
Rural Fire Protection (proposed legislation)	—	7,000	—	—
Urban and Community Forestry	—	1,200	—	—
Alaska Native Claims Settlement Act	—	1,047	—	—
Forestry Incentives (proposed legislation)	—	10,000	—	—

APPENDIX 5-2 continued

Appropriation Item	FY 1973 Appropriation	FY 1974 Forest Service Requests	FY 1974 Department of Agriculture Request	FY 1974 President's Budget (OMB Request)
SUBTOTAL—APPROPRIATED FUNDS				
Budget authority	527,930	686,103	402,797	369,272
Program level	—	886,303	538,667	452,773
PERMANENT APPROPRIATIONS				
Expenses, Brush Disposal:				
Budget authority	18,000	15,000	18,000	18,000
Program level	—	18,538	19,157	19,157
Roads and Trails for States (10% Fund)	33,871	36,400	38,500	40,900
Forest Fire Prevention:				
Budget authority	215	250	250	250
Program level	—	275	275	275
Restoration of Forest Lands and Improvements:				
Budget authority	50	50	50	50
Program level	—	50	50	50
Payment to Minnesota	259	260	259	259
Payments to Counties, National Grasslands	524	554	549	549
Payments to School Funds, Arizona and New Mexico	114	75	115	115
Payments to States, National Forests Fund	84,676	90,800	96,012	102,012
TOTAL PERMANENT APPROPRIATIONS				
Budget authority	137,709	143,389	153,735	162,135
Program level	137,709	146,952	154,917	163,317
COOPERATIVE WORK, FOREST SERVICE (*trust fund*):				
Budget authority	54,000	43,000	55,000	55,000
Program level	—	46,632	50,348	50,348
GRAND TOTAL:				
Budget authority	719,639	872,492	611,532	586,407
Program level	—	1,079,887	743,932	666,438.9

Source: Forest Service, "Agency Budget Estimates for Fiscal Year 1974" (Jan. 29, 1973), and Hearings before a Subcommittee on Appropriations, *Department of the Interior and Related Agencies Appropriations for Fiscal Year 1974*, 93d Cong., 1st Sess., Part 3, pp. 2152–2153 (1973).

Status of Financing Development Program for the National Forests
Fiscal Years 1963–1972 (in Thousands)

The planned levels shown in this table were developed by the Forest Service and were not specifically indicated in the program submitted by the President on September 21, 1961. This program stated that it would "be carried out as rapidly as possible within overall budgetary requirements and financial resources of the Federal Government."

	1963–1972 Planned Level[1]	1963–1972 Available				
		Forest Service Appropriation[1]	Public Works	Total[1]	Difference	Percent Financed
FOREST LAND MANAGEMENT:						
National Forest Protection and Management:						
Timber resource management:						
(a) Sales administration and management	$392,584	$388,286		$388,286	$4,298	98.9
(b) Reforestation and stand improvement	451,907	182,439	$5,294	187,733	264,174	41.5
Recreation-public use	786,060	335,414	10,611	346,025	440,035	44.0
Wildlife habitat management	72,926	42,894	1,637	44,531	28,395	61.1
Range resource management:						
(a) Management	74,136	58,586		58,586	15,550	79.3
(b) Revegetation	34,503	29,755	46	29,801	4,702	86.4
(c) Improvements	51,379	36,649	1,986	38,635	12,744	75.2

APPENDIX 5-3 continued

	1963–1972 Available					
	1963–1972 Planned Level[1]	Forest Service Appropriation[1]	Public Works	Total[1]	Difference	Percent Financed
Soil and water management	124,970	63,680	1,206	64,886	60,084	51.9
Mineral claims, leases, and special uses	49,938	42,921		42,921	7,017	85.9
Land classification, adjustments, and surveys	90,663	55,684		55,684	34,979	61.4
Forest fire protection	381,549	264,564	1,187	265,751	115,798	69.7
Maintenance of improvement for fire and general purposes (including communications)	185,303	101,762	16,715	118,477	66,826	63.9
TOTAL, NATIONAL FOREST PROTECTION AND MANAGEMENT	2,695,918	1,602,634	38,682	1,641,316	1,054,602	60.9
Insect and Disease Control	129,154	115,427	197	115,624	13,530	89.5
Acquisition of Lands, Weeks and Special Acts	68,497	16,682		16,682	51,815	24.4
Forest Roads and Trails (including all related appropriations) (obligating authority)	1,509,133	1,166,716	18,719	1,185,435	323,698	78.6
TOTALS	4,402,702	2,901,459	57,593	2,959,057	1,443,645	67.2

[1] Includes following amounts appropriated under Construction and Land Acquisition:
Recreation-public use $9,463,000
Construction and maintenance of improvement for fire and general purposes 3,168,000
Acquisition of lands 1,300,000
Note: The planned level figures include increased pay costs for classified employees. They do not include such items as effects of inflation on contract costs, wage board rates, material and equipment costs, etc.
Source: U.S. Department of Agriculture, Forest Service, Budget Branch, April 11, 1972.

Notes

CHAPTER 1

1. Robert A. Marshall, *The People's Forests* (New York: Smith and Haas, 1933), pp. 79–80.
2. Hearings before a Subcommittee of the House Committee on Appropriations, *Department of the Interior and Related Agencies Appropriations for 1974*, 93rd Congress, 1st Session, Part 1, pp. 430–431 (1973); U.S. Mining Laws (16 U.S.C. §§ 22–47).
3. Hearings before the Subcommittee on Public Lands of the Senate Committee on Interior and Insular Affairs, *"Clear-Cutting" Practices on National Timberlands*, 92nd Congress, 1st Session, Part 1, p. 297 (1971).
4. Letters to Ralph Nader from Herbert Snyder, Secretary of the National Council of Public Land Users, Grand Junction, Colo., June 17, 1972, and Daniel Smiley, Portal, Ariz., November 29, 1971. See James Nathan Miller, "The Nibbling Away of the West." *Reader's Digest* (December 1972).
5. Knutson-Vandenberg Act of 1930 (16 U.S.C. § 576).
6. Interview by Daniel R. Barney with Walker P. Newman, Division of Timber Management, Forest Service, June 22, 1972. [All interviews were conducted in Washington, D.C., and all references to the Forest Service are to the Chief's Office, Forest Service, U.S. Department of Agriculture, Washington, D.C., unless otherwise noted.]
7. House Hearings, *op. cit.*, Part 1, p. 292; Forest Service, "Programmable Backlog Reforestation Needs on National Forests," prepared by Walker P. Newman, Division of Timber Management, Forest Service (June 21, 1972); interview with Walker P. Newman, *op. cit.*
8. Forest Service, *Quality in Timber Management—A Current Evaluation* (Missoula, Mont.: Northern Region, 1970); Forest Service, *Forest Management in Wyoming* (Ogden, Utah: Wyoming Forest Study Team, 1971); studies by the Forest Service in California and Georgia are referred to in U.S. General Accounting Office, *Additional Actions Needed to Minimize Adverse Environmental Impacts of Timber Harvesting and Road Construction on Forest Land*, Report No. B-125053 to the Congress by the Comptroller General of the United States (Washington, D.C., 1973).
9. Environmental Protection Agency, *Industrial Waste Guide on Logging Practices*, prepared by one of EPA's forerunners, the Federal Water Pollution Control Administration, U.S. Department of the Interior (Portland, Ore., 1970).
10. See Forest Service, "FALCON [Forestry, Advanced Logging, and CONservation]—A Research and Development Program for Advanced Logging Systems" (1972). The freezing of $5 million in fiscal year 1973 appropriations for FALCON by the President's Office of Management and Budget has brought this promising program to a standstill. Letter to Daniel R. Barney from Gene S. Bergoffen, Director of Legislative Affairs, Forest Service, April 10, 1973.

159

11. U.S. General Accounting Office, *op. cit.*, p. 1.
12. Forest Service, "A Forest Service Environmental Program for the Future" (September 1970, revised April 1971, revised January 1972).
13. Creative Act of 1891 (16 U.S.C. § 471).
14. Weeks Law (16 U.S.C. §§ 480, 500, 513–519, 521, 552, 563).
15. Land and Water Conservation Fund Act of 1965 (16 U.S.C. § 460l (4)).
16. See Appendix I-5, "Forest Service Fact Sheet," and House Hearings, *op. cit.*, Part 1, p. 406ff.
17. House Hearings, *op. cit.*, Part 1, pp. 414–415; for comparison of National Park and National Forest recreation use figures, see U.S. Department of the Interior, Bureau of Outdoor Recreation, *Selected Outdoor Recreation Statistics, 1971* (1971), Table D-5, p. 58.
18. Forest Service, *The Outlook for Timber in the United States: A Report of the Findings of the 1970 Timber Review*, review draft (December 5, 1972), Table 2–13.
19. FSM [*Forest Service Manual,* the compendium of directives from the Chief of the Forest Service to his subordinates; accessible to the public at the offices of forest supervisors, regional foresters, and the Chief] 2412.14.3 (May 1972).
20. Forest Service, *op. cit.*, note 18 *supra*, Table 1–17; Forest Service, *Douglas-fir Supply Study* (Portland, Ore.: Pacific Northwest Forest and Range Experiment Station, 1969), pp. 3, 4, 45.
21. Transfer Act of 1905 (16 U.S.C. §§ 472, 524, 554).
22. Organic Administration Act of 1897 (16 U.S.C. § 475).
23. Gifford Pinchot, *Breaking New Ground* (New York: Harcourt–Brace, 1947).
24. Interview by James S. Henry, Nader Study Group, with Clark Row, Chief of Forest Economics Branch, Division of Forest Economics and Marketing Research, Forest Service, July 8, 1970.

CHAPTER 2

1. Hearings before the Subcommittee on Housing and Urban Affairs of the Senate Committee on Banking, Housing and Urban Affairs, *Shortages and Rising Prices of Softwood Lumber*, 93rd Congress, 1st Session, p. 678 (1973).
2. Hearings before the Subcommittee on Public Lands of the Senate Committee on Interior and Insular Affairs, *"Clear-Cutting" Practices on National Timberlands*, Part 1, p. 81 (1971).
3. National Forest timber harvest was 805,375,000 board feet in 1920, and 1,740,271,000 board feet in 1940 [telephone interview by Daniel R. Barney with James W. Thorne, Division of Timber Management, Forest Service, July 24, 1972]. Total U.S. timber production was 59,175,000,000 board feet in 1920, and 54,325,-000,000 board feet in 1940 [Forest Service, *Timber Trends in the United States* (February 1965), Table 47, p. 219].
4. Interview by Daniel R. Barney with Murl W. Storms, Chief of Forestry, Bureau of Land Management, U.S. Department of the Interior, June 13, 1972.
5. "Potential Net Growth Per Acre in South, North, Pacific Coast, and Rocky Mountains," table compiled by Robert W. Larson, Division of Forest Economics and Marketing Research, Forest Service, May 1972.
6. Forest Service, *Timber Resources for America's Future* (January 1958), Table 82, p. 135; Forest Service, *The Outlook for Timber*

in the United States: A Report of the Findings of the 1970 Timber Review, review draft (December 5, 1972), Table 1-17.

7. *Ibid.*, Table 2–7.
8. *Ibid.*, "Highlights"; tables 2–13 and 2–14; pp. 2–22, 2–28, 2–49ff.
9. Forest Service, *Douglas-fir Supply Study* (Portland, Ore.: Pacific Northwest Forest and Range Experiment Station, 1969), pp. vii, 4.
10. Forest Service, *California's Forest Industries—Prospects for the Future*, USDA Forest Service Resource Bulletin PNW-35 (Portland, Ore., Pacific Northwest Forest and Range Experiment Station, 1970), pp. 11, 23, 24, 25. For a similarly pessimistic forecast, see Forest Service, *The Timber Resources of Humboldt County, California*, USDA Forest Service Resource Bulletin PNW-26 (Portland, Ore.: Pacific Northwest Forest and Range Experiment Station, 1968).
11. Forest Service, *The Outlook for Timber in the United States, op. cit.*, Table 2-14.
12. *Forest Industries* (April 1973), p. 32.
13. Forest Service, *Douglas-fir Supply Study, op. cit.*, Table 5, p. 43.
14. "Major Forest Product Companies in the United States," prepared by the American Forest Institute, Washington, D.C. (July 1972). Companies counted are those listed in "Lumber and Wood Products" (36,795 firms), "Furniture and Fixtures" (10,008), and "Paper and Allied Products" (5,890) categories in U.S. Department of Commerce, Bureau of the Census, *Statistical Abstract of the United States, 1972*, 93rd edition (1972), Table No. 1188, p. 708.
15. Forest Service, *The Outlook for Timber in the United States, op. cit.*, Table 2-13.
16. U.S. Department of Commerce, *op. cit.*, Table No. 1188, p. 709.
17. Information prepared by the American Forest Institute, Washington, D.C. (May 3, 1972), on the basis of Forest Service statistics.
18. Forest Service, *Douglas-fir Supply Study, op. cit.*, Table 4, p. 42. For another grim prediction of the impact of overcutting on employment in the Northwest, see Louis Hamill, *A Forecast of the Forest Resource and Industry of Douglas and Lane Counties* (Eugene, Ore.: Bureau of Business Research, University of Oregon, 1963), p. xxi.
19. Forest Service, *Douglas-fir Supply Study, op. cit.*, p. 41.
20. 116 Cong. Rec. 5117 (1970).
21. Foreign Assistance Act of 1968 (16 U.S.C. § 617); Hearings before the Senate Select Committee on Small Business, *Timber Management Policies*, 90th Congress, 2nd Session, p. 146 (1968).
22. S. 1033, 93rd Congress, 1st Session (1973); Senate Hearings, *Shortages and Rising Prices of Softwood Lumber, op. cit.*
23. S. 350, 92nd Congress, 1st Session (1971). See Hearings before the Subcommittee on Public Lands of the Senate Committee on Interior and Insular Affairs, *Management Practices on Public Lands*, 92nd Congress, 1st Session, Parts 1–3 (1971).
24. Forest Service, "Statement of John R. McGuire, Associate Chief, Forest Service, U.S. Department of Agriculture, before the Subcommittee on Public Lands of the Committee on Interior and Insular Affairs, United States Senate, on S. 350, The American Forestry Act, and S. 1734, The Forest Lands Restoration Act, on March 10, 1972" (1972).

25. Forest Service, "Estimated Value of Timber Products Harvested in the United States, 1970" (1970).

26. Frederick L. Webber, a former employee of the National Forest Products Association, was Congressman Dellenback's administrative assistant in 1970. He is presently Special Assistant for Legislative Affairs to President Nixon.

27. Letter from George C. Cheek, Executive Vice President, American Forest Institute, Washington, D.C., to Daniel R. Barney, April 3, 1972.

28. FPPEC contributions to Congressional and Senatorial candidates in 1966, 1968, and 1970, are listed in letters from Henry Bahr, Treasurer of FPPEC, to the Clerk, U.S. House of Representatives, dated: January 3, 1967; April 3, 1968; July 1, 1968; October 2, 1968; October 25, 1968; November 1, 1968; December 31, 1968; March 31, 1970; July 6, 1970; September 8, 1970; October 21, 1970. A list of 1972 campaign contributions is available on microfilm, filed under "Forest Products Political Committee," in the office of the Secretary of the United States Senate. See also "List of 1970 Disclosures by Members of the Senate," *CQ Fact Sheet*, (Washington, D.C.: Congressional Quarterly, Inc., May 24, 1971), p. 11.

29. "Comparative Political Activity," chart prepared by the Forest Products Political Education Committee, Washington, D.C. (1970).

30. "A Partnership for Progress," prepared by the National Forest Products Association, Washington, D.C. (March 1972).

31. Statement by William J. Connolly, Vice President, International Paper Company, quoted in Albert W. Wilson, "Image-Building Campaign Urged for Forest Industry," *Pulp & Paper* (March 1972), p. 80.

32. "Forest Industries Council 1972–74 Communications Program" (Washington, D.C.: Forest Industries Council, June 19, 1972), p. 2-1ff.

33. *Ibid.*, p. 1-1.

34. Printed in *Saturday Review* (*The Society*) (September 16, 1972) and other national publications.

35. Forest Service, "Explanatory Notes—FY 1967 Budget" (1966), p. 14.

36. See Ralph D. Hodges, Jr., "A Program to Improve Lumber and Plywood Availability" (Washington, D.C.: National Forest Products Association, December 27, 1968).

37. S. 1775, 93rd Congress, 1st Session (1973); Hearings on S. 1775 before the Subcommittee on Environment, Soil Conservation, and Forestry of the Senate Committee on Agriculture and Forestry, 93rd Congress, 1st Session (June 26 and 27, 1973); "Lumber: Through the Roof," *Newsweek* (April 2, 1973); Statement of John T. Dunlop, Director, Cost of Living Council, Senate Hearings, *Shortages and Rising Prices of Softwood Lumber, op. cit.*, p. 49ff; Cost of Living Council News Release, CLC-270 (May 29, 1973); plaintiffs' papers filed in *Natural Resources Defense Council, Inc. v. Butz*, Civil No. 1358-73 (D.D.C., filed June 22, 1973).

38. Lumber and wood products constitute 16.6 percent of the construction cost of an average single-family dwelling [Franklin E. Williams, "Material Requirements for Single-Family Houses," *Construction Review*, U.S. Department of Commerce, Bureau of Domestic Commerce (February 1972), p. 7], which in 1971, equalled $23,866 (median). The fully financed cost of an

average single-family dwelling, $45,600, was obtained by mul-
tiplying the median "Monthly Payment to Principal and In-
terest" of the single-family home owner, $152, by 12 months,
and by 25 years (the life of most mortgages) ["Section 203b-1
Family Homes," *FHA Trends of Home Mortgage Characteristics
(Fourth Quarter 1971)*, U.S. Department of Housing and
Urban Development, Housing Production and Mortgage Credit–
FHA (May 25, 1972), pp. 8, 10].

39. Senate Hearings, *"Clear-Cutting" Practices on National Timberlands, op. cit.*, Part 3, p. 949.

40. For a discussion of the lumber supply crisis, see Hearings before the Subcommittee on Forests of the House Committee on
Agriculture, *National Timber Supply Act of 1969*, 91st Congress,
1st Session (1969). Hearings before the Subcommittee on Soil
Conservation and Forestry of the Senate Committee on Agriculture and Forestry, *National Timber Supply Act*, 91st Congress, 1st Session (1969); Senate Document No. 91-27, *Effect
of Lumber Prices and Shortages on the Nation's Housing Goals*,
91st Congress, 1st Session (1969).

41. In January 1969, at the height of the lumber supply crisis, the
Forest Service noted in a letter to the National Association of
Home Builders that insufficient timber yield from the National
Forests was not necessarily the cause of the crisis, as the National Forest Products Association was claiming. After all, it
pointed out, the timber companies could have eased lumber
shortages by harvesting the huge backlog of uncut National
Forest timber under contract—a step they had refrained from
taking up to that point: "Nationwide we estimate that we have
37.5 billion board feet of uncut timber under contract. When
this is discounted by the long-term pulp contracts we have in
Alaska, there remains 26.6 billion board feet [*the equivalent of
2.3 years of annual cut*, since actual cut for the entire National
Forest System in fiscal year 1969 was 11.8 billion board feet]
of uncut sawtimber under contract. Most of this timber was
put under contract 2 to 5 years ago, at price levels which could
not have acted to cause the lumber price spiral which started
12 months ago. While an unknown amount of this uncut timber
may not yet be roaded and cannot be operated now, *it does
serve to indicate that solution to the short-range supply and
price problem does not lie entirely on the National Forests*."
[emphasis added] Letter from A. W. Greely, Associate Chief of
the Forest Service, to Joseph McGrath, Vice President of the
National Association of Home-Builders, Washington, D.C., January 10, 1969. Current backlog figures are in Forest Service,
"National Forest Timber Sale Accomplishments for Fiscal Year
1972" (March 22, 1973), p. 1.

42. Interview by Daniel R. Barney with John Muench Jr., Forest
Economist, National Forest Products Association, Washington,
D.C., June 14, 1972.

43. Forest Service, *The Outlook for Timber in the United States,
op. cit.*, Chapter 4, "Availability of World Timber Resources."

44. 36 C.F.R. § 221.2 (1972), as amended by 38 Fed. Reg. 20326
(1973).

45. Forest Service, *op. cit.*, note 43 *supra*, pp. I-65ff, 3-67ff, 5-137ff.

46. National Academy of Sciences, "Policies for Solid Waste Management," prepared for the Office of Solid Waste Management,
Environmental Protection Agency (Washington, D.C.: 1970).

47. Bank of America, N.T. & S.A., "Paper Recycling: A Report on

Its Economic and Ecological Implications" (San Francisco, Ca., December 1971), p. 3.

48. Wayne F. Carr [Chemical Engineer, Forest Products Laboratory, Forest Service, Madison, Wisconsin], "Many Problems Involved in Increasing Utilization of Waste Paper," *Paper Trade Journal* (May 17, 1971), p. 50.

49. "Potential Net Growth Per Acre in South, North, Pacific Coast, and Rocky Mountains," *op. cit.*

50. Forest Service, *The Outlook for Timber in the United States, op. cit.*, pp. 3-15.

51. *Ibid.*, pp. 3-16.

52. Hearings before a Subcommittee of the House Committee on Appropriations, *Department of the Interior and Related Agencies Appropriations for 1974*, 93rd Congress, 1st Session, Part 1, p. 532ff (1973).

53. Forest Service, *The Outlook for Timber in the United States, op. cit.*, Chapter 3, "Opportunities for Increasing Timber Supplies Through Intensified Management and Utilization."

54. *Ibid.*, pp. 3-34.

55. Hearing on S. 3105 and S. 3459 before the Subcommittee on Environment, Soil Conservation, and Forestry of the Senate Committee on Agriculture and Forestry, *Forestry Programs*, 92nd Congress, 2nd Session, p. 11ff (1972).

56. Letter from Thomas K. Cowden, Assistant Secretary of Agriculture, to U.S. Senator Herman E. Talmadge, Chairman of the Senate Committee on Agriculture and Forestry, April 17, 1972, reprinted in *ibid.*, p. 3. Senate Report No. 92-856, 92nd Congress, 2nd Session (1972); S. 3105 passed the Senate, June 15, 1972; a similar bill was introduced in the House but was not considered by committee before the 92nd Congress adjourned. H.R. 12873, 92nd Congress, 2nd Session (1972).

57. Southern Forest Resources Analysis Committee, *The South's Third Forest* (Atlanta, Ga.: Southern Forest Institute, 1969).

58. *Ibid.*, pp. 47–48.

59. The president of the industry's Southern Forest Institute lamented the industry's sluggish response to the report, when he spoke to the Institute's 1973 meeting. Reported in Richard W. Bryan, "Industry Admonished—'3-F' Pace Lagging," *Forest Industries* (April 1973), p. 32.

60. Letter to Daniel R. Barney from Rexford A. Resler, Associate Chief, Forest Service, March 19, 1973.

61. Gerald S. Gilligan, "Timberland: How Much Should You Own?" *Pulp & Paper* (December 1972), p. 84.

62. Forest Service, *The Outlook for Timber in the United States, op. cit.*, Table 2-7.

63. Gerald S. Gilligan, "Timberland Ownership: How Profitable Is It?" *Pulp & Paper* (January 1973), p. 76.

64. 16 U.S.C. § 406l (4).

65. Interview by Daniel R. Barney with Lyle McDowell, Chief of Park Operations, National Park Service, U.S. Department of the Interior, June 13, 1972.

66. Robert A. Marshall, *The People's Forests* (New York: Smith and Haas, 1933).

67. U.S. Department of the Interior, Bureau of Outdoor Recreation, *Outdoor Recreation Trends* (April 1967), p. 18.

68. U.S. Department of the Interior, National Park Service, *Forecast of Visits to the National Park System, 1972–1976 and 1981* (Winter 1972), p. 1.

69. U.S. Department of the Interior, Bureau of Outdoor Recreation, *Selected Outdoor Recreation Statistics* (March 1971), Table D-5, p. 58.
70. Forest Service, "Recreation Use Projections, 1970–1980," prepared by John Butt, Division of Program and Policy Analysis, and Gordon Sanford, Division of Recreation, Forest Service (June 1971); House Hearings, *Department of the Interior and Related Agencies Appropriations for 1974, op. cit.*, Part 1, pp. 414–415.

CHAPTER 3

1. As quoted by Michael Frome, Conservation Editor of *Field & Stream*, in testimony given before the House Subcommittee on Forests: Hearing before the Subcommittee on Forests of the House Committee on Agriculture, *Establish a Commission to Investigate Clearcutting of Timber on Public Lands*, 92nd Congress, 2nd Session, p. 36 (1972).
2. Dale A. Burk, *The Clearcut Crisis* (Great Falls, Mont.: Jursnick Printing Co., 1970), pp. 11, 13. This book is a compilation of State Editor Burk's muckraking articles on the Bitterroot controversy in the Missoula, Montana, *Missoulian* during late 1969.
3. *Ibid.*, pp. 20, 22.
4. *Ibid.*, p. 63.
5. Letter to Daniel R. Barney from Paul E. Neff, Director of Timber Management, Forest Service, October 25, 1972.
6. Forest Service, *Management Practices on the Bitterroot National Forest* (Missoula, Mont.: Forest Service Northern Region–Intermountain Station Task Force, 1970), p. 29.
7. Senate Document No. 91-115, *A University View of the Forest Service*, prepared for the Senate Committee on Interior and Insular Affairs by a Select Committee of the University of Montana, 91st Congress, 2nd Session, p. 14 (1970).
8. Memorandum from Steve Yurich, Regional Forester, Northern Region, Forest Service, to Orville Daniels, Forest Supervisor, Bitterroot National Forest, July 26, 1971.
9. Letter to Daniel R. Barney from Orville L. Daniels, Forest Supervisor, Bitterroot National Forest, June 14, 1972.
10. Forest Service, "Bitterroot National Forest Multiple Use Plan, Part I" (Hamilton, Mont., 1972); Forest Service, "USDA Forest Service Environmental Statement: Multiple Use Plan— Moose Creek Planning Unit, Bitterroot National Forest" (Hamilton, Mont., 1973); Forest Service, "USDA Forest Service Draft Environmental Statement: Upper West Fork Planning Unit, Bitterroot National Forest" (Hamilton, Mont., 1973).
11. West Virginia House of Delegates Concurrent Resolution No. 26, February 5, 1970; West Virginia Forest Management Practices Commission, *Report on Forest Management Practices on National Forest Lands in West Virginia*, prepared for the West Virginia Legislature (August 1, 1970); testimony of numerous prominent West Virginians on the controversy in Hearings before the Subcommittee on Public Lands of the Senate Committee on Interior and Insular Affairs, *"Clear-Cutting" Practices on National Timberlands*, 92nd Congress, 1st Session, Part 1 (1971).
12. Letter to Daniel R. Barney from U.S. Senator Jennings Randolph, December 11, 1972. Also see Letter to U.S. Senator Jennings Randolph from Frederick A. Dorrell, Forest Super-

visor, Monongahela National Forest, April 16, 1969; Forest
Service, *Even-Age Management on the Monongahela National
Forest*, prepared by the Chief's Special Review Committee
(Washington, D.C., 1970); letter to Daniel R. Barney from
Robert A. Schirck, Range, Wildlife and Timber Staff Officer,
Monongahela National Forest, May 31, 1972.

13. At press time, the federal court had just decided in favor of the
conservationists. *Izaak Walton League* v. *Butz*, 6 ERC 1016
(N.D.W.Va. Nov. 6, 1973).

14. Hearings before a Subcommittee of the Senate Committee on
Appropriations, *Department of the Interior and Related Agen-
cies Appropriations for Fiscal Year 1971*, 91st Congress, 2nd
Session, Part 3, p. 3038 (1970).

15. Forest Service, *Forest Management in Wyoming* (Ogden, Utah:
Wyoming Forest Study Team, 1971), p. 5.

16. Senate Hearings, *"Clear-Cutting" Practices on National Timberlands, op. cit.*, Parts 1–3.

17. Hearings before the Subcommittee on Public Lands of the Senate Committee on Interior and Insular Affairs, *Management
Practices on Public Lands*, 92nd Congress, 1st Session, Parts
1–3 (1971).

18. Senate Committee on Interior and Insular Affairs Committee
Print, "An Analysis of Forestry Issues in the First Session of
the 92nd Congress," 92nd Congress, 2nd Session pp. 53–61
(April 1972).

19. Senate Hearings, *"Clear-Cutting" Practices on National Timberlands, op. cit.*, Part 1; Senate Hearings, *Management Practices
on Public Lands, op. cit.*, Parts 1–3.

20. S. 1734, 92nd Congress, 1st Session (1971).

21. Leon Minkler, Gordon Robinson, Peter Twight, and Charles
Stoddard, "Dominant Use-Clearcutting versus Conservative
Forestry and Multiple Use" (Duluth, Minn.: Northern Environ-
mental Council, 1972).

22. *American Forests* (February 1973).

23. Letter to U.S. Senator Jennings Randolph from Frederick A.
Dorrell, *op. cit.*

24. Forest Service, *Management Practices on the Bitterroot National
Forest, op. cit.*, pp. 9–10.

25. Forest Service, *Even-Age Management on the Monongahela National Forest, op. cit.*, p. 22.

26. Letter to Daniel R. Barney from L. W. Deitz, Citizen Member
of the West Virginia Forest Management Practices Commission
and past President of the Richwood Chamber of Commerce,
Richwood, W. Va., May 24, 1972.

27. Letters to Daniel R. Barney from U.S. Senator Jennings Randolph, May 10, 1972, and December 11, 1972.

28. Forest Service, *National Forest Management in a Quality Environment—Timber Productivity* (1971).

29. Forest Service, *National Forests in a Quality Environment—
Action Plan* (1972).

30. *Ibid.*, p. 5.

31. *Ibid.*, p. 7.

32. Letter to Daniel R. Barney from Dale A. Burk, State Editor of
Missoula, Montana, *Missoulian*, May 27, 1972. For further indi-
cations of the Montana public's continuing dissatisfaction with
Bitterroot management, see the letters reprinted in Forest Ser-
vice, "USDA Forest Service Environmental Statement: Multiple
Use Plan—Moose Creek Planning Unit, Bitterroot National
Forest," *op. cit.*

33. Richard M. Alston, *FOREST—Goals and Decisionmaking in the Forest Service,* USDA Forest Service Research Paper INT-128 (Ogden, Utah: Intermountain Forest and Range Experiment Station, 1972), pp. 51–52.

34. FSM 2111.5 (Emergency Directive No. 1, Forest Service Manual, Washington, D.C., November 9, 1971); Forest Service, "Inform and Involve" (1972); Forest Service, "A Guide to Public Involvement" (1972).

35. National Environmental Policy Act of 1969 (42 U.S.C. § 4332); FSM 1940 (Emergency Directive No. 1, Title 1900, Forest Service Manual, July 13, 1971).

36. *West Va. Highlands Conservancy* v. *Island Creek Coal Co.,* 441 F.2d 232 (4th Cir. 1971); *Sierra Club* v. *Butz,* 3 ELR 20071 (N.D. Calif. Dec. 11, 1972), *appeal docketed,* No. 73-1646, 9th Cir., Apr. 11, 1973; *Wyoming Outdoor Coordinating Council* v. *Butz,* 484 F.2d 1244 (10th Cir. 1973); *MinnPIRG* v. *Butz,* 358 F. Supp. 584 (D. Minn. 1973); *Izaak Walton League* v. *Butz,* 6 ERC 1016 (N.D.W. Va. Nov. 6, 1973); *Natural Resources Defense Council, Inc.* v. *Butz,* Civil No. 1358-73 (D.D.C., filed June 22, 1973).

37. Elizabeth Peelle, "Forest Management and Land Use Conflicts: A Case Study of Resource Management," prepared under the Oak Ridge National Laboratory–National Science Foundation Environmental Program and presented at the National Commission on Materials Policy and Georgia Institute of Technology University Forum Conference, June 26–28, 1972, Atlanta, Ga., p. 16.

38. Forest Service, *Management Practices on the Bitterroot National Forest, op. cit.,* p. 9.

39. Forest Service, *The Outlook for Timber in the United States: A Report of the Findings of the 1970 Timber Review,* review draft (December 5, 1972), "Highlights"; Tables 2–13 and 2–14; pp. 2–22, 2–28, 2–49ff.

40. Congressional Research Service, "Summary of the Five Reports on Clearcutting Prepared for the President's Council on Environmental Quality, With Emphasis on Policy Recommendations," in Senate Committee on Interior and Insular Affairs Committee Print, *op. cit.,* pp. 29–49.

41. Interview by Daniel R. Barney with William T. Lake, Counsel, Council on Environmental Quality, Executive Office of the President, June 23, 1972.

42. Council on Environmental Quality, "Position Paper—Timber Harvesting on the Public Lands" (November 11, 1971), pp. 1, 3.

43. Senate Subcommittee on Public Lands, "Clearcutting on Federal Timberlands," in Senate Committee on Interior and Insular Affairs Committee Print, *op. cit.,* pp. 53–61.

44. Press release from the Office of the White House Press Secretary, San Clemente, California (September 2, 1971); "Statement by the President on the Report of the Task Force of the Cabinet Committee on Economic Policy, June 19, 1970," *Weekly Compilation of Presidential Documents* (June 22, 1970), pp. 787–790.

45. Council on Environmental Quality, [draft] "Executive Order: Environmental Guidelines for Timber Harvesting on the Public Lands" (as finally revised, January 12, 1972).

46. *Ibid.*

47. "Answers to Questions of the Senate Appropriations Subcommittee on Agriculture, Environment, and Consumer Protection," prepared by the Council on Environmental Quality (Spring 1972), p. 3.

48. Interview by Daniel R. Barney with William T. Lake, *op. cit.*
49. Both Joseph B. McGrath, Vice President of the National Forest Products Association, Washington, D.C., and Secretary Butz himself have verified this account: interview by Daniel R. Barney with Joseph B. McGrath, June 15, 1972; testimony of Earl Butz, Secretary of Agriculture, at Hearings before a Subcommittee of the Senate Committee on Appropriations, *Agriculture-Environmental and Consumer Protection Appropriations for Fiscal Year 1973*, 92nd Congress, 2nd Session, Part 1, p. 40 (1972).
50. Interview by Daniel R. Barney with William T. Lake, *op. cit.*
51. Senate Hearings, *Agriculture-Environmental and Consumer Protection Appropriations for Fiscal Year 1973, op. cit.*, Part 1, p. 42.
52. E. W. Kenworthy, "Limit on Cutting Timber Dropped," *New York Times* (January 14, 1972); Daniel Schorr, "Transcript of Clearcutting Story," *CBS Evening News* (January 14, 1972), CBS News, Washington, D.C.
53. Senate Hearings, *Agriculture-Environmental and Consumer Protection Appropriations for Fiscal Year 1973, op. cit.*, pp. 41–42.
54. Interview by Daniel R. Barney with William T. Lake, *op. cit.*
55. "A Too Clear-Cut Decision," editorial, *New York Times* (January 18, 1972).
56. Gifford Pinchot, *Breaking New Ground* (New York: Harcourt–Brace, 1947).
57. Michael Frome, *The Forest Service* (New York: Praeger, 1971), Chapters 1-3.
58. Peelle, *op. cit.*, p. 27.
59. Forest Service, *Even-Age Management on the Monongahela National Forest, op. cit.*, p. 21.
60. See extensive testimony by scientists and others in Senate Hearings, *"Clear-Cutting" Practices on National Timberlands, op. cit.*, Parts 1 and 2; also, F. H. Bormann *et al.*, "Nutrient Loss Accelerated by Clear-Cutting of a Forest Ecosystem," *Science* (February 23, 1968); G. E. Likens *et al.*, "Effects of Forest Cutting and Herbicide Treatment on Nutrient Budgets in the Hubbard Brook Watershed-Ecosystem," *Ecological Monographs* (Winter 1970); Frederick E. Smith, "Ecological Demand and Environmental Response," *Journal of Forestry* (December 1970); Donald H. Gray, "Effects of Forest Clearcutting on the Stability of Natural Slopes," *Bulletin of the Association of Engineering Geologists* (Fall 1970).
61. Forest Service, "Research Testimony Presented at Church Hearing," memorandum from John R. McGuire, Deputy Chief, Forest Service, to Regional Foresters, Directors, and Area Directors, Forest Service (June 16, 1971).
62. Robert Zahner statement in *ibid.*, p. 54.
63. Senate Hearings, *"Clear-Cutting" Practices on National Timberlands, op. cit.*, p. 63.
64. Irvin C. Reigner, "Water from the Forests," *Water Spectrum* (1970), reprinted in *ibid.*, p. 903.
65. Senate Hearings, *"Clear-Cutting" Practices on National Timberlands, op. cit.*, pp. 115, 314; Burk, *op. cit.*, p. 26.
66. The Bolle Committee's initial conclusion that clearcutting in most of the Bitterroot National Forest could not be justified on economic grounds (Senate Document No. 91–115, *op. cit.*) has been separately substantiated in far greater detail: Robert A. Bennett, *A Cost and Yield Comparison of Alternative Harvesting Methods on Selected Forest Vegetation Types in the Bitter-*

root *National Forest,* unpublished thesis, presented in partial fulfillment of the requirements for the degree of Master of Science in Forestry, University of Montana (Missoula, Mont., 1973). Bennett concludes that the harvesting method with the lowest cost and highest return is selection cutting (p. 85).

67. Leon Minkler *et. al., op. cit.;* Statement of Peter A. Twight, then Administrative Assistant for Forestry, National Parks & Conservation Association, Washington, D.C., in House Hearings, *op. cit.,* p. 72.

CHAPTER 4

1. As reported in Nancy Wood, *Clearcut!* (San Francisco: Sierra Club Battlebooks, 1971).
2. Forest Service, *Forest Regulation Study,* preliminary draft (March 1973), p. 4.
3. See text at notes 16–20, *infra.*
4. Multiple Use–Sustained Yield Act of 1960 (16 U.S.C. §§ 529, 531); Organic Administration Act of 1897 (16 U.S.C. § 551).
5. 16 U.S.C. § 531.
6. 16 U.S.C. § 475.
7. 36 C.F.R. §§ 221.6, 221.3(a) (1972).
8. The *Forest Service Manual* and related Forest Service Handbooks are published in the Office of the Chief by the Division of Administrative Management for use by all Forest Service units. *Manual* and Handbook directives are supplemented in the field offices by the Regional Forester, Forest Supervisor, and other officials. 36 C.F.R. § 200.4 (1972).
9. FSM 2412 (May 1972).
10. FSM 2413 (May 1972).
11. Interviews by Daniel R. Barney with Robert Wambach, Dean and Professor of Forestry, and Richard Behan, Professor of Forestry, School of Forestry, University of Montana, conducted in Missoula, Montana, on July 29, 1973, and July 26, 1973, respectively. "Affidavit of Gordon Robinson [Staff Forester, Sierra Club, San Francisco, Ca.; former chief forester, Southern Pacific Co., San Francisco, Ca.]," *Natural Resources Defense Council, Inc., v. Butz,* Civil No. 1358–73 (D.D.C., filed June 22, 1973).
12. FSM 2415.2 (May 1972).
13. FSM 2415.41 (May 1972).
14. 36 C.F.R. § 221.3(a)(5) (1972); FSM 2415.42 (May 1972).
15. FSM 2410.3 (Emergency Directive No. 16, Washington, D.C., May 1, 1973).
16. "Affidavit of Gordon Robinson," *op. cit.; Sierra Club v. Hardin,* 325 F.Supp. 99 (1971), *motion for remand for a new trial sub nom. Sierra Club v. Butz,* 3 E.L.R. 20292 (9th Cir., March 16, 1973).
17. Forest Service, *Stratification of Forest Land for Timber Management Planning on the Western National Forests* (Ogden, Utah: Intermountain Forest and Range Experiment Station, 1971), p. 4.
18. Forest Service, *Forest Regulation Study, op. cit.,* p. 4.
19. Forest Service, "Allowable Harvest, Timber Sold and Timber Harvested, F.Y. 1960 thru 1971," prepared by the Division of Timber Management (March 22, 1972); Forest Service, "National Forest Timber Sale Accomplishments for Fiscal Year 1972," prepared by Division of Timber Management (March 22, 1973).

20. Forest Service, *Management Practices on the Bitterroot National Forest* (Missoula, Mont.: Northern Region, 1970), pp. 9, 64.
21. 16 U.S.C. §§ 528–531.
22. Forest Service, *Forest Regulation Study, op. cit.*, p. 5.
23. In the case of a national emergency proclaimed by the President of the United States, "temporary overcutting of the approved allowable cut is authorized to the extent necessary to meet needs created by the emergency." FSM 2410.41 (May 1972).
24. Forest Service, "A Forest Service Environmental Program for the Future" (September 1970, revised April 1971, revised January 1972). A narrative of the plan's origin follows later in this chapter.
25. *Ibid.*, p. 10; Memorandum, "Special Task Force on Lumber Prices," from B. H. Payne, then Associate Deputy Chief, Forest Service, to Chief and Staff, Forest Service, August 13, 1969. See note 51, *infra.*
26. Telephone interview by Daniel R. Barney with Adrian Gilbert, Director of Program and Policy Analysis, Forest Service, March 27, 1973. Also see Memorandum, "Forest Service Environmental Program for the Future," from J. W. Deinema, Associate Deputy Chief, Forest Service, to Division Directors, NFS [National Forest System], enclosing "Objectives for Phase II, Environmental Program for the Future," draft (April 6, 1971, revised September 24, 1971), October 5, 1971.
27. Paul E. Neff [Director of Timber Management, Forest Service], "Calculation of Allowable Harvest for the National Forests," *Journal of Forestry* (February 1973), p. 86ff.
28. Forest Service, *The Outlook for Timber in the United States: A Report of the Findings of the 1970 Timber Review*, review draft (December 5, 1972), Chapter 3.
29. Letter to Daniel R. Barney from H. R. Josephson, Director of Forest Economics and Marketing Research, Forest Service, March 8, 1973.
30. S. 1832, 91st Congress, 1st Session (1969); H.R. 10344, 91st Congress, 1st Session (1969).
31. In early 1969, the Forest Service saw the timber supply bill for the first time when it received a draft copy "from a timber purchaser." [Memorandum from Homer J. Hixon, then Director of Timber Management, Forest Service, to the Regional Foresters, Forest Service, February 20, 1969.] Late in December 1968, Forest Service officials received the first reports from the field that a timber supply bill was in the works, and that the "timber people were getting stirred up all over the place." [Interview by Hale Andrews, Nader Study Group, with A. W. Greeley, then Associate Chief of the Forest Service, July 7, 1970.] For a sensitive and comprehensive probe into the Forest Service's role in the National Timber Supply Act debate, see Hale Andrews, "The United States Forest Service and the Timber Supply Act of 1969," unpublished paper prepared for the Center for Study of Responsive Law, Washington, D.C. (September 1970).
32. Hearings before the Subcommittee on Forests of the House Committee on Agriculture, *National Timber Supply Act of 1969*, 91st Congress, 1st Session, p. 93 (1969).
33. Hearings before the Subcommittee on Soil Conservation and Forestry of the Senate Committee on Agriculture and Forestry,

National Timber Supply Act, 91st Congress, 1st Session, p. 16 (1969).

34. Forest Service, "Statement of John R. McGuire, Associate Chief, Forest Service, U.S. Department of Agriculture, before the Subcommittee on Public Lands of the Committee on Interior and Insular Affairs, United States Senate, on S. 350, the American Forestry Act, and S. 1734, The Forest Lands Restoration Act, on March 10, 1972" (1972); Testimony of John R. McGuire, Chief, Forest Service, before the Subcommittee on Environment, Soil Conservation, and Forestry of the Senate Committee on Agriculture and Forestry, at hearing on S. 1775, 93rd Congress, 1st Session, June 26, 1973.

35. Forest Service, "Comments on *The Last Stand*," enclosed in letter to Daniel R. Barney from John R. McGuire, Chief, Forest Service, May 14, 1973; 116 Cong.Rec. 5103-5104 (1970).

36. 116 Cong.Rec. 5117 (1970).

37. "Determination of Yield for FARR (10 Year)," draft report prepared by Robert W. Pearl, Division of Timber Management, Forest Service (May 21, 1969), Appendix I.

38. "Opportunities for Timber Management Intensification on the National Forests," report prepared by Robert Marty and Walker P. Newman, Division of Timber Management, Forest Service, October 29, 1968. The first reference to the 7-billion-board-foot increase, which was based on the 1968 study, was in Memorandum, "Special Task Force on Lumber Prices," from B. H. Payne, then Associate Deputy Chief, Forest Service, to Saul Nelson, Chairman, Working Group of the Presidential Task Force on Softwood Lumber and Plywood, March 12, 1969.

39. Working Group of the Presidential Task Force on Softwood Lumber and Plywood, "Lumber and Plywood Working Party, Second Report," April 3, 1969, Forest Service Files.

40. Forest Service, "Possibilities for Meeting Future Demands for Softwood Timber in the United States," prepared for the Working Group of the Cabinet Task Force on Lumber (August 1, 1969; revised September 29, 1969), p. 16.

41. Memorandum, "Findings and Recommendations of Task Force on Softwood Lumber and Plywood," from Robert P. Mayo, then U.S. Budget Director and Chairman, Presidential Task Force on Softwood Lumber and Plywood, to the Cabinet Committee on Economic Policy, October 24, 1969.

42. Memorandum from Charles W. Colson, Special Counsel to the President, to Robert P. Mayo, Chairman, Presidential Task Force on Softwood Lumber and Plywood, and then Budget Director, April 17, 1970.

43. "Determination of Yield for FARR (10 Year)," *op. cit.,* Appendix I.

44. "Justification for Administrative Approach," prepared by "the timber people," attached to Memorandum from Charles W. Colson to Robert P. Mayo, *op. cit.*

45. Memorandum, "Meeting of Working Group of Task Force on Softwood Lumber and Plywood," from B. H. Payne, then Associate Deputy Chief, Forest Service, to The Record (files), April 29, 1970.

46. "Statement by the President on the Report of the Task Force of the Cabinet Committee on Economic Policy, June 19, 1970," *Weekly Compilation of Presidential Documents* (June 22, 1970), pp. 787–790.

47. Letter, "Re: Timber Supply Act of 1969 (H.R. 12025)," to his

fellow Members of Congress, from U.S. Representative John P. Saylor, June 23, 1970.

48. Forest Service, "A Forest Service Environmental Program for the Future," *op. cit.*

49. Forest Service, "Search for Solitude" (June 1970), Frontispiece.

50. Interview by Daniel R. Barney with Robert A. Rowen, Chief of Special Areas Branch, Division of Recreation, Forest Service, July 14, 1972; Memorandum from B. H. Payne to Chief and Staff, *op. cit.*

51. "The effect [of the proposed acceleration in timber production] on conversion period [i.e., the period during which the old-growth is completely removed and replaced with new, young trees] is estimated as follows:

"Acres of old-growth in R [Forest Service Regions] 1-6	52.6 million acres
Area cut annually	565,000 acres
Volume cut annually	9.7 billion b.f.
Present conversion period (52.6 million acres/ 565,000 acres)	93 years
Average volume per acre (9.7 billion b.f./ 565,000 acres)	17 million b.f.

*   *   *

"At the middle level, the target is an increase of 8 billion board feet, made up of 7.4 billion board feet from the National Forests and the remainder from other public lands.

"At the middle level, we would produce 7.4 billion board feet over the '69 level (13.8) as follows:

"Current allowable cut	13.64 [billion b.f.]
Thinning and salvage	2.19
Intensification practices, i.e., reforestation, T.S.I., etc. (Actual old-growth harvest)	3.42
Use of present unregulated in Lower 48 States	1.19
and in Alaska	0.56
Subtotal (Excl. of A.C.)	7.36 [billion b.f.]
"To produce 3.42 billion b.f., we would cut [an additional]	201,000 acres [per year]
"This would reduce the conversion span to 69 years, a reduction of	24 years."

Memorandum from B. H. Payne to Chief and Staff, *ibid.*

52. Memorandum, "Appraisal of Output Targets for 1980," from Joseph Pechanec, then Director, Intermountain Forest and Range Experiment Station, Ogden, Utah, Forest Service, to John R. McGuire, then Deputy Chief, Forest Service, January 14, 1970.

53. Memorandum from B. H. Payne to Saul Nelson, *op. cit.*

54. Memorandum, "Development Program for Forest and Related Resources," from W. J. Lucas, Chairman, FARR Task Force, Forest Service, to Washington Office Division Directors, Forest Service, April 18, 1969.

55. Memorandum, "Program for Forests and Related Resources," from W. J. Lucas to Division Directors, Forest Service, April 28, 1969.

56. Memorandum from T. F. McLintock, Director of Forest Insect and Disease Research, Forest Service, to W. J. Lucas, May 1, 1969.
57. Memorandum from L. P. Neff, Assistant Director of Recreation, Forest Service, to Richard J. Costley, Director of Recreation, Forest Service, May 7, 1969.
58. Memorandum from Richard J. Costley to W. J. Lucas, May 7, 1969.
59. Memorandum from Henry DeBruin, then Director of Information and Education, Forest Service, to W. J. Lucas, May 8, 1969.
60. Memorandum from W. O. Hanson, Division of Wildlife Management, to W. J. Lucas, May 12, 1969.
61. Memorandum from Homer J. Hixon, then Director of Timber Management, Forest Service, to W. J. Lucas, May 27, 1969.
62. Memorandum from William J. Hurst, Regional Forester, Southwestern Region, to John R. McGuire, then Deputy Chief, Forest Service, March 11, 1970.
63. Memorandum from Joseph Pechanec to John R. McGuire, *op. cit.*
64. Memorandum from Robert P. Mayo to Cabinet Committee on Economic Policy, *op. cit.,* p. 2.
65. Memorandum, "Findings and Recommendations of Task Force on Softwood Lumber and Plywood," from Edward P. Cliff, then Chief of Forest Service, to T. K. Cowden, Assistant Secretary of Agriculture, October 30, 1969.
66. Letter from Henry Drummonds, Nader Study Group, to Edward P. Cliff, Chief, Forest Service, July 28, 1970.
67. Letter from Art Merriman, Assistant Director of Information and Education, Forest Service, to Henry Drummonds, August 14, 1970.
68. Memorandum, "Response to BOB Issue Paper—Timber Price Outlook for 1972 & the later 1970's," from Homer J. Hixon to B. H. Payne, April 17, 1970.
69. Forest Service, "A Forest Service Environmental Program for the Future," *op. cit.,* p. 10.
70. Draft Report, "Combined Draft of Material Prepared for Task Force (FARR) Report to Working Group," by W. J. Lucas and John Fedkiw, Deputy Director, Office of Planning and Evaluation, Department of Agriculture, to Working Group (September 19, 1969), p. 3.
71. Forest Service, "Proposed New Wilderness Study Areas" (January 1973), pp. 1–2; Forest Service, "Search for Solitude," *op. cit.*
72. Letter from Brock Evans, Northwest Representative, Sierra Club, Seattle, Washington, to Henry Drummonds, July 15, 1970. According to Robert A. Rowen, the Forest Service's wilderness administrator, the Forest Service has information to verify or contradict the Sierra Club's assertion only in its regional offices, if it has *any* information on the subject of Primitive Area reclassification [Interview with Robert A. Rowen by Daniel R. Barney, *op. cit.*].
73. Interview with Arthur Smith, Attorney, Division of Lands and Natural Resources, U.S. Department of Justice, by Daniel R. Barney on July 18, 1972 [Smith frequently acts as counsel for the Forest Service in litigation involving the agency].
74. Wilderness Act of 1964 (16 U.S.C. § 1131).
75. House Document No. 92-156, 92nd Congress, 1st Session, p. 3 (1971).
76. Forest Service, "National Forest Primitive Area Review—Status

2-25-72" (1972); Forest Service, "Proposed New Wilderness Study Areas," *op. cit.*

77. *Parker v. United States*, 309 F.Supp. 593 (D.Colo. 1970), affirmed 448 F.2d 793 (10th Cir. 1971), certiorari denied, 405 U.S. 989 (1972).

78. Forest Service, "Comments on *The Last Stand*," *op. cit.*

79. 16 U.S.C. § 1131; *Parker v. United States*, 448 F.2d 793 (10th Cir. 1971).

80. Council on Environmental Quality, "Executive Order _____: Protection of Areas Eligible for Inclusion in National Wilderness Preservation System," draft, April 16, 1971.

81. Interview by Daniel R. Barney with William T. Lake, Counsel, Council on Environmental Quality, June 26, 1972.

82. Telephone interview by Daniel R. Barney with Robert A. Rowen, Chief of Special Areas Branch, Division of Recreation, Forest Service, July 21, 1972.

83. "Major Conservation Opportunities for the Pacific Northwest," report prepared by Brock Evans, then Northwest Representative, Sierra Club, Seattle, Wash., January 1972.

84. Hearings before the Subcommittee on Public Lands of the Senate Committee on Interior and Insular Affairs, *"Clear-Cutting" Practices on National Timberlands*, 92nd Congress, 1st Session, Part 1, p. 346 (1971).

85. The 11 states contain 1,031,430 million board feet of timber in their softwood National Forests, including 34,000 million board feet in Wilderness Areas and 16,000 million board feet in Primitive Areas [Memorandum, "Questions from Nader's Office," from F. Leroy Bond, Associate Director of Timber Management, Forest Service, to Henry Drummonds, June 29, 1970].

86. "Major Conservation Opportunities for the Pacific Northwest," *op. cit.;* Senate Hearings, *National Timber Supply Act, op. cit.*, pp. 73–74.

87. Letter from Brock Evans, Northwest Representative of the Sierra Club, Seattle, Washington, to Daniel R. Barney, December 27, 1971.

88. *Ibid.*

89. 16. U.S.C. § 1131.

90. FSM 2321 (January 1967).

91. 16 U.S.C. § 1131.

92. FSM 2321 (May 1969); 2321.1, 2321.12, 2312.13 (January 1967).

93. Council on Environmental Quality, *op. cit.*

94. Memorandum, "Coordination," from Edward P. Cliff, Chief, Forest Service, to Regional Foresters, Forest Service, February 26, 1971.

95. Forest Service, "Comments on *The Last Stand*," *op. cit.*

96. Interview by Daniel R. Barney with James Freeman, Staff Assistant for Land Use Planning, National Forest System, Forest Service, July 14, 1972.

97. Telephone interview with Robert A. Rowen, *op. cit.*

98. *Sierra Club v. Butz*, 3 ELR 20071 (N.D. Calif., Dec. 11, 1972). *appeal docketed*, No. 73-1646, 9th Cir., Apr. 11, 1973.

99. *Id.* Memorandum, "Roadless Area Review," from E. W. Schultz, Acting Chief, Forest Service, to Regional Foresters, November 28, 1972. The Natural Resources Defense Council, Palo Alto, California, obtained a court ruling extending the impact statement requirement to roadless areas on which timber cutting contracts had been signed prior to the filing of the Sierra Club suit

in June 1972. *Wyoming Outdoor Coordinating Council* v. *Butz,* 484 F.2d 1244 (10th Cir. 1973).

100. Various timber companies intervened in the suit as co-defendants with the Secretary of Agriculture, claiming that a decision in favor of the plaintiff conservation groups would cause them tremendous monetary damage through breaches of timber cutting contracts.

101. 16 U.S.C. § 1131; Interview with Robert A. Rowen, *op. cit.*

102. Forest Service, "Statement of John R. McGuire, Chief, Forest Service Department of Agriculture, before the Subcommittee on Public Lands of the Committee on Interior and Insular Affairs, United States Senate, on S. 316, relating to Eastern Wilderness, on February 21, 1973" (February 1973). pp. 6–7.

103. Interview by Daniel R. Barney with John R. McGuire, Chief, Forest Service, June 21, 1972.

104. 16.U.S.C. § 1131.

105. Quoted in George Alderson, "Eastern Wilderness Crisis," *Environmental Quality* (March 1973), p. 70.

106. Compare Sections 2(c) and 4(c), 16 U.S.C. § 1131.

107. S. 316, 93rd Congress, 1st Sesssion (1973).

108. Draft bill attached to letter to the Speaker, U.S. House of Representatives, from J. Phil Campbell, Under Secretary of Agriculture, February 21, 1973.

109. Alderson, *op. cit.*, p. 72.

110. *Ibid.*

111. Interview by Daniel R. Barney with Ralph D. Hodges, Jr., Executive Vice President, National Forest Products Association, Washington, D.C., December 12, 1972, in Cambridge, Mass.

112. Forest Service, "Proposed New Wilderness Study Areas," *op. cit.*, p. 2.

CHAPTER 5

1. Charles A. Reich, "Bureaucracy and the Forests," Center for the Study of Democratic Institutions, Santa Barbara, Ca., in Hearings before the Subcommittee on Public Lands of the Senate Committee on Interior and Insular Affairs, *"Clear-Cutting" Practices on National Timberlands,* 92nd Congress, 1st Session, Part 2, p. 722 (1971).

2. Quoted in George Alderson, "Eastern Wilderness Crisis," *Environmental Quality* (March 1973), p. 42.

3. Hearings before a Subcommittee of the Senate Committee on Appropriations, *Department of the Interior and Related Agencies Appropriations for Fiscal Year 1974,* Part 3, p. 2152 (1973).

4. Forest Service, "Comments on *The Last Stand,*" enclosed in letter to Daniel R. Barney from John R. McGuire, Chief, Forest Service, May 14, 1973.

5. Chronicled in Michael Frome, *The Forest Service* (New York: Praeger, 1971), pp. 190–191.

6. Chapter 13—"Where Does the Forest Service Belong?" *ibid.* Also, Forest Service, "The Forest Service: How It Fits in the Federal Structure" (June 1969); Hearings before the Senate Committee on Government Operations, *Establish a Department of Natural Resources,* 92nd Congress, 1st Session, Part 3 (1971).

7. See Appendix 5-1, "Forest Service Budget Estimates and Appropriations, FY 1955–1972," and 5-2, "Forest Service Appropriations, FY 1973."

8. Forest Service, "Available Appropriations and Amounts Placed in Reserve for Fiscal Year 1973" (1973).

9. James Risser, "The U.S. Forest Service: Smokey's Strip Miners," *Washington Monthly* (December 1971), p. 16.

10. Hearings before a Subcommittee of the House Committee on Appropriations, *Department of the Interior and Related Agencies Appropriations for 1974,* 93rd Congress, 1st Session, Part 1, p. 409 (1973).

11. 16 U.S.C. §§ 500, 501 (1970).

12. 16 U.S.C. § 528 (1970).

13. Hearings before the Subcommittee on Forests of the House Committee on Agriculture, *National Forests—Multiple Use and Sustained Yield,* 86th Congress, 2nd Session, p. 39 (1960).

14. 16 U.S.C. § 460 l (4) (1970).

15. Forest Service, "Development Program for the National Forests," Miscellaneous Publication No. 896 (November 1961).

16. Forest Service, *Management Practices on the Bitterroot National Forest* (Missoula, Mont.: Northern Region, 1970), p. 14.

17. Richard M. Alston, *FOREST—Goals and Decisionmaking in the Forest Service,* USDA Forest Service Research Paper INT-128 (Ogden, Utah: Intermountain Forest and Range Experiment Station, 1972), p. 70.

18. 16 U.S.C. § 516 (1970).

19. Forest Service, "National Forest System Areas as of June 30, 1972" (1972).

20. Forest Service, "Guide for Managing the National Forests in the Appalachians" (Atlanta, Ga.: Southern Region, 1971), pp. 7, 33.

21. *Ibid.*, p. 8.

22. Si Kahn, "The National Forests and Appalachia" (Mineral Bluff, Ga.: Cut Cane Associates, 1973), p. 2.

23. *McCaysville Citizen* (McCaysville, Ga.), September 23, 1971.

24. Tennessee Valley Authority, "TVA Power: Payments in Lieu of Taxes" (Knoxville, Tenn.: TVA Information Office, November 1972).

25. *Ibid.*

26. U.S. Department of Health, Education, and Welfare, Office of Education, *Administration of Public Laws 81–874 and 81–815: 20th Annual Report of the Commissioner of Education* (June 30, 1970), Introduction, p. 1.

27. As noted by Si Kahn, Mineral Bluff, Ga., at a "listening session" on the Cohutta Mountains Unit by the Forest Service in Chatsworth, Ga., August 1, 1972.

28. Appalachian Regional Commission, "Appalachian Region Poverty Trend Data by County, 1970 and 1960" (1973).

29. *Atlanta Constitution* (Atlanta, Ga.), May 12, 1971.

30. *Blue Ridge Summit-Post* (Blue Ridge, Ga.), October 11, 1972.

31. *Ibid.*

32. *McCaysville Citizen,* September 23, 1971.

33. *Ibid.*

34. Forest Service, "Inform and Involve" (February 1, 1972).

35. *Ibid.*, p. 18ff.

36. Hearings before the Subcommittee on Forests of the House Committee on Agriculture, *Establish a Commission to Investigate Clearcutting of Timber on Public Lands,* 92nd Congress, 2nd Session, p. 92 (1972).

37. Reich, *op. cit.*, p. 712.

38. FSM 2130 (April 1967).

39. Forest Service, *Even-Age Management on the Monongahela Na-*

tional Forest (Washington, D.C.: Chief's Special Review Committee, 1970), p. 23.

40. Forest Service, *Stratification of Forest Land for Timber Management Planning on the Western National Forests,* USDA Forest Service Research Paper INT-108 (Ogden, Utah: Intermountain Forest and Range Experiment Sttaion, 1971), p. 22.

41. Forest Service, *Forest Management in Wyoming* (Wyoming Forest Study Team, 1971), p. 69.

42. Forest Service, *Management Practices on the Bitterroot National Forest, op. cit.,* p. 10.

43. FSM 2100 (Emergency Directive No. 1, Washington, D.C., November 9, 1971).

44. FSM 2111.3 (November 9, 1971); Telephone interview by Daniel R. Barney with Warren Walters, Multiple Use Planning and Coordination, California Region, Forest Service, San Francisco, Ca., July 5, 1973. See the EPA's comments on a typical unit plan: Letter to Orville L. Daniels, Forest Supervisor, Bitterroot National Forest, Hamilton, Mont., from John A. Green, Regional Administrator, Environmental Protection Agency, Denver, Colo., in Forest Service, "USDA Forest Service Environmental Statement: Multiple Use Plan—Moose Creek Planning Unit" (Hamilton, Mont.: Bitterroot National Forest, 1973). Concerning the "multiobjectives," see FSM 2121 (November 9, 1971); 36 Fed.Reg. 24150 (1971).

45. FSM 2123.26 (November 9, 1971).

46. FSM 2111.5 (November 9, 1971).

47. Reich, *op. cit.,* pp. 721–722.

CHAPTER 6

1. Gifford Pinchot, *Breaking New Ground* (New York: Harcourt–Brace, 1947), p. 287.

2. Forest Service, "Bitterroot National Forest Multiple Use Plan, Part I" (Hamilton, Mont.: Bitterroot National Forest, 1972), pp. 4–5.

3. Forest Service, *Friday Newsletter* (September 18, 1970).

Index